The Light of Learning

Activating Our Divine Possibilities

The Light of Learning

Activating Our Divine Possibilities

by Robert R. Leichtman, M.D.
& Carl Japikse

ARIEL PRESS
Atlanta — Columbus

No Royalties Are Paid on This Book

This book is made possible
by anonymous gifts
to the Publications Fund of Light

ISBN 0-89804-170-8

Table of Contents

To

All Members

of Light

Past, Present, and Future

Introduction

An Agent of Light

The path to enlightenment begins with an understanding—the understanding that we are a being of light. We possess, on loan, bodies of flesh, feeling, and thought, but these are only temporary residences. The real home of our selfhood is a body of light. Our bodies of flesh, feeling, and thought serve their function, and then they pass, but our true nature in light does not pass. Neither does it fail.

We are made as spirit; spirit is the cause of our being and all which happens to us. This spirit is a spark of divine energy; as it seeks expression as an individual, the spark glows and radiates, producing light. This is not physical light, which is feeble and dim, but the light of consciousness: immortal, unlimited, and creative. It is the substance of our humanity, the wellspring of our individuality, talent, wisdom, love, courage, and joy.

It is important to recognize this inner nature of light and

distinguish it from the form and activity of the personality. Since we are a being of light, we ought to be inspired by this light, motivated by this light, and healed by this light. Yet often we are not.

The problem is one of becoming aware of our true identity. Through many eons, the light—which is our true self—has projected its radiance into the shadows of form, seeking to illumine that which is obscured. In the process, however, our personal sense of identity, which should be filled with light, has been blurred; we have identified with the shadows. We have come to think of ourself in terms of our experiences, perceptions, reactions, hurts, achievements, and associations—instead of as light. The poet Robert Frost captures this dilemma poignantly:

> I have been one acquainted with the night.
> I have walked out in rain—and back in rain.
> I have outwalked the furthest city light.
> I have looked down the saddest city lane.
> I have passed by the watchman on his beat
> And dropped my eyes, unwilling to explain.

To properly honor the light within us, we must look beyond the night. We must renew our acquaintance with light. Primarily, this means identifying with the soul and its plans, rather than the personality, with its wants, complaints, and difficulties.

An analogy which helps illustrate why this is important is the nature of physical light as it expresses itself through a light bulb. The bulb is the form through which the light shines, and yet it is not light. Nor can it produce light by itself. Only when it is connected to a source of electricity can the light bulb actually give off light.

Unless connected with spirit, our personality is no better able to produce the light it is designed to express than a light bulb that is not connected with electricity. Enlightenment is never produced in the personality alone; it is the result of integrating the daily life of the personality with the purposes and life of spirit.

It is this dynamic interplay which causes the light of our being to shine in the physical world.

Enlightenment has little to do with being able to see white light, "open the third eye," or run white light energy up and down the spine. Instead, the enlightened individual is one who is focused in the light of the soul and is able to sustain that focus through his daily self-expression. The hallmarks of enlightenment are mastery of the emotions, the ability to comprehend issues of life which are confusing and complex to others, and the capacity to work creatively in life.

It should be obvious, therefore, that the single most important step toward enlightenment is the effort to make the personality a more fit vehicle for the light of God. Enlightenment is. the product primarily of the effort to express our talent, wisdom, love, courage, and joy as fully as possible in our daily activities. Or, to put this idea a little more poetically, enlightenment is achieved by learning to breathe in and breathe out the light of the soul. We breathe in the light by attuning ourself to the ideals of life and filling our awareness, our appreciation, and our adoration with these ideals. We breathe out the light by seeking to invest these same ideals in all that we do—in our work, relationships, hobbies, and recreation.

In all these endeavors, our goal must be to unite the events and needs of the personality with the actual light of the soul. This involves four basic stages:

1. **Discovering the light.** It may be tempting to dismiss this stage of enlightenment as trivial, but it is not. Long after the personality intellectually and emotionally recognizes that there is a soul and its nature is light, it still insists on substituting something less than real in lieu of light. In confronting a difficult relationship, for example, the personality may go through the motions of consulting the soul as to how to proceed—and then block out the light and do what it prefers anyway. And yet the self-deception is accepted; the personality contentedly believes it is fulfilling the desires of the soul, even while gratifying its own wishes and whims.

To *discover* the light, therefore, we must begin by carefully distinguishing between the light and shadow. Light impels us to grow. It leads us into paths of rightness. It causes us to increase our skills, our understanding, and our compassion. It is found in our highest aspirations, ideals, values, and maturity—never in our wishes and good feelings.

2. **Comprehending the light.** Once the light is discovered, it must be understood and rightly interpreted. This stage is not an easy one to master, as light is multidimensional by nature. It cannot be understood only in three-

dimensional terms; the study of light forces us to think in terms of immortality and infinity as well. It forces us to give up one limitation of thought after another.

Understanding the nature of our personal destiny is a good example of this difficulty. It frequently occurs that certain events befall us that make little sense in the context of our work, needs, or other activities. The personality is often confused by these events, and may even question the wisdom of a soul which could let them happen. It may doubt the benevolence of the light itself. Such doubts and puzzlements, however, are simply signs of incomprehension. The vastness of light has escaped our narrow view. Inevitably, such circumstances do fit a larger pattern of continuity, either helping us learn a lesson we have been studiously ignoring for a long time, or preparing us for opportunities as yet unseen in the shadows of daily life—but perfectly obvious in the light of spirit.

Another example of the difficulty of comprehending the light is the difference between the conventional expressions of the ideals of love, joy, beauty, and wisdom and their actual realities in light. All too often, for example, the expression of love is marred by sentimentality, possessiveness, and jealousy. Enlightened love, however, has nothing to do with these distortions.

Thus, to *comprehend* light, we must seek always to look for the higher perspective which makes sense of our feelings, attitudes, challenges, and conflicts. When light is properly comprehended, it removes all doubt, second-guessing, and confusion.

3. Integrating the light. At the level of the soul, we are a

11

being of light, but the personality remains in shadow. The third stage of enlightenment, consequently, is the integration of the light of the soul with the needs and activities of the personality, so that our daily self-expression radiates light as well. In practical terms, this means blending the light of our love, joy, courage, and wisdom into the unredeemed or imperfect elements of our attitudes, habits, values, talents, and activities.

As the path to enlightenment is trod, the crabby, blighted, mean, and ignorant areas of our personality slowly ebb away, and are replaced by light. We treat others better than before. We view ourself with more dignity; we act with a greater measure of gracefulness. We eliminate our tendencies toward carelessness, dishonesty, and laziness. In this way, we become a more effective person, by ridding ourself of that which does not embody the light.

This is not a matter of accommodation, where we layer a thin icing of niceness over an otherwise hostile and selfish personality. As Jesus put it, "No one can serve two masters." It is not possible to serve the light and the shadow both; therefore, to *integrate* the light into the personality, we must remove all traces of shadow. We must purge that which is impure and welcome into our consciousness that which will honor the light. We must harmonize the personality with the plans and purposes of the soul.

4. Expressing the light. Again Jesus said, "Men do not light a lamp and put it under a bushel, but on a stand, so it gives light to all in the house. Let your light so shine before all men, that they may see your good works and give glory to your Father who is in heaven." The work of enlighten-

12

ment is a private undertaking between the personality and the soul, but the fruits of enlightenment must be shared with all. Light is radiant; it is against its nature to be contained and held private. If we are not working to express light in all we do and think and say, we are not really dealing with light at all—just a glimmer.

We *express* the light by building with it, serving with it, and healing with it. Light seeks to create; as we become creative, even in humble ways, we express the light. Light seeks to serve; as we contribute to its service, we express the light. Light seeks to heal; as we focus its healing warmth, for the benefit of others, ourself, and civilization, we express the light.

Usually this creativity, serving, and healing is far from spectacular. It is carried out quietly, without fanfare, in the context of our work, relationships, interests, and social responsibilities. By striving to enlighten life and leave it a little better than we found it, we express light.

These four stages of the process of enlightenment apply not just to individuals, of course, but to the groups and institutions of humanity as well. Churches, governments, science, and civilization need enlightenment as well as individuals. So do education, literature, business, the arts, and many other significant avenues of human endeavor. The same principles apply. Little is gained just by polishing up the shadowed forms of these institutions or enterprises, through the infusion of large amounts of money or worry. What is required is a genuine perception of the lighted ideal within these endeavors, a comprehension of how that light can best be honored, hard work in harmonizing the group involved with the direction of light, and continued effort to express the highest measure of light possible.

If we persevere, the reward is great. We become an agent of light.

The lessons in the *Enlightenment* series all deal with this theme—becoming an agent of light. The intent is to demonstrate what it means to discover the light, comprehend it, integrate that light into the life of the personality, and express it in all we think, do, and say.

In their original form, the lessons of light were grouped in seven categories. Each lesson covered a topic from one specific category. This book, *The Light of Learning,* is a compilation of the fourteen lessons from *Enlightenment* that deal with the topic of learning. The other six categories present lessons that are still being written. These six categories are:

• The nature of archetypal forces and symbols and how they express light through religion, mythology, literature, music, and the events of individual life.

• Self-expression and why it is important, with lessons on the male/female principles, creativity, healing, the enlightened work ethic, and group expressions.

• Integration—of soul and personality, the mind and emotions, values and self-expression, and the individual with groups.

• Enriching the mind—through reading, appreciation of the arts, interaction with the fourth and fifth dimensions, observation of life, and interpretation of dreams and meditations.

14

• Exploring the psychic worlds and understanding the nature of astral ecology, mass consciousness, and group minds of all sorts.

• Interacting with other kingdoms of life and discerning the value of their relationship with humanity, thereby expanding our awareness of the full scope of divine life.

Enlightenment is a call to action, not just fodder for further intellectual study. Becoming an agent of light is an active process, requiring the direct involvement of the individual seeking enlightenment. We must understand that all elements of life are suitable targets for the work of enlightenment; only as we individualize the light does it radiate through our own life.

We do not need to become a missionary in Africa to find light—or retire to a monastery or ashram and ape the movements of saints. Our work, hobbies, relationships, responsibilities, and efforts to grow are the suitable and proper vehicles for light. They provide us rich opportunity for discovering the light, comprehending it, integrating it, and expressing it. Unless we focus the light through these activities, whatever they may be, we will not really be doing its work.

There is no moment too insignificant to use this formula. After all, if we cannot be an agent of light in the midst of annoyance or pettiness or simple fatigue, it is hardly reasonable to expect to be an agent of light in more spectacular circumstances. If we cannot be faithful in a little, it is foolish to believe we could be faithful over much. If we cannot heal, build, and serve with light, even in the smallest of ways, we cannot rightly expect to be healed, strengthened, or served by the light ourself. Therefore, to receive light, we must learn to contribute light. To be enlightened, we must become an agent of light.

Which prepares us for becoming the light itself.

1.

An Enlightened Philosophy of Education

To be an agent of light, we must become a master of learning; the very nature of light demands it. Light impels us to grow, individually and collectively. It leads us to new discoveries—about nature, ourself, and the inner dimensions of life. It inspires us with creative ideas and teaches us new modes of thinking. Light helps us acquire the skills and talents we need in order to make our way in the world; it reveals the divine principles of life and encourages us to translate them into mature ethics, values, convictions, and behavior. Indeed, light is the dynamic factor in all learning, all growth.

Unfortunately, learning is an activity most of us take for granted. We think of it as an occupation for the young and ignorant, which loses its importance as we become older and, as the cliché claims, wiser. We also tend to regard learning as automatic: that if we study the right books or attend the right lectures, we will absorb knowledge—and amassing knowledge, we believe, is the goal of education.

Because we have made these assumptions about learning, we have become dependent, individually and as a culture, on our teachers. We go to someone to learn, and give him or her the responsibility to educate us. We accept his or her curriculum, guidance, and limitations. Nowhere is this passivity more apparent than in those spiritual aspirants who search for a guru to enlighten them, or in religious devotees who expect the priests of their faith to save them. But it infiltrates the whole of society and has greatly narrowed the impact of education. It has caused us to look for education only in schools and universities, and has led us to believe that education is something which is done to us, rather than something we do for ourself.

Learning is actually designed to be a lifelong endeavor, as much a natural part of our daily activity as eating and breathing. The highest sign of intelligence in a human being is his or her *willingness to learn*, and that is just as relevant for a person who is forty-five or seventy-five as it is for someone who is fifteen. The greatest sign of stupidity, by contrast, is the refusal of anyone at any age to learn something new—or to believe he does not need to pursue further education.

Moreover, learning is a personal responsibility. Schools, universities, and teachers can be a great source of assistance, but that is all they should be regarded as. They are not the embodiment of education; only the individual can be that. The principal teacher for each of us is the light within us, our higher self. Learning is a process of growing toward this light, just as the flowers of the garden grow toward the sun. Unlike the plants, however, we do not grow automatically; learning is not an instinct, but an obligation. It is an obligation to seek out the inner light and consult it frequently. For we are both teacher and learner together and must recognize the significance of this relationship. Once we do, then we have discovered something vital about learning—and about the nature of light.

Truly, it can be stated that the respect we have for the light of learning, and the value we accord it, will influence everything else we do in life. If we are dedicated to the pursuit of learning, we will breathe new life and growth into every sphere of our interest and activity. But if we are committed to remaining "as is," and do not seek to become someone better, our life will stagnate and grow dark.

It is therefore important to develop an enlightened philosophy of education and use it to guide and direct our unfoldment as a human being.

What is education? To the average person, it is the process of learning certain facts and skills, of acquiring training which will lead to greater success in a career, or of progressing through graded levels of instruction and receiving a degree. It is inextricably associated with tests, teachers, and textbooks.

To the agent of light, however, education is much more. The word "education" means "to draw forth," and in its classical origins, it referred to the process of drawing forth the light of one's spirit—the light of one's love, wisdom, talent, and creativity. This meaning has largely been lost in modern traditions of education—but it very much needs to be restored.

In this context, education is the process of learning to express the life of the soul more completely in everything we do. For the child, it means preparing him to recognize and implement the full range of physical, emotional, and mental skills and qualities—and become responsive to the inner light. For the adult, it means learning to integrate the life of the soul into the daily activities of work, responsibility, and recreation.

Practical examples of approaching education in this way would include:

• Learning to be a more enlightened parent, by becoming more responsive to the light within our children, by developing a more mature expression of love, and by mastering better self-discipline.

• Learning to express our emotions more effectively, by teaching ourself to draw forth the best emotional qualities within us—compassion, dignity, courage, tolerance, and poise—and express them in our daily life.

• Learning to think with greater wisdom, by practicing the skills of intelligence—discernment, the interpretation and use of symbolic thought, intuition, logic, and most importantly, common sense.

• Learning to broaden our sense of responsibility, in the contributions we make at work, in our duties as a citizen, and in our obligations to the life of spirit.

Few of these lessons are found in textbooks, or taught in schools. But this does not deter the agent of light, who sees

20

every moment in life as an opportunity to learn. This does not mean that he views experience as the great teacher, for experience can actually be, and frequently is, a great deceiver. Rather, it means that he regards *light itself* as the great teacher, textbook, and test.

Esoterically, this is a statement of profound meaning. Light, or consciousness, is the second aspect of God—the divine capacity for love and wisdom. Education is that process which helps us prepare and train the personality to know and express this divine love and wisdom. As we learn, we become filled with light. We develop a more mature use of the body, emotions, and mind, and integrate these three vehicles of form into a coherent, stable, and inspired personality—a personality which is integrated with its inner light.

The whole work of education, therefore, can be meaningfully expressed in terms of light.

First, education is that process which helps us become more aware of the existence and nature of light. This can be as the direct result of spiritual training about the soul and the divine nature of the universe, but it can be less mystical as well. Science, for example, teaches us some of the great principles of natural law—and these certainly help us become aware of light. The study of psychology likewise can inform us of many aspects of the nature of man; the study of literature can lead us to develop intuitive skills of thinking; the study of mathematics can guide us in sharpening our logic. All of these disciplines therefore embody elements of light; indeed, all of life's phenomena can reveal the presence of light, if we are willing to study them and learn from them. But to be successful in this endeavor, we must start with the assumption that it is light which inspires these phenomena in the first place.

Second, education helps us learn the skills of expressing light. These skills cover a very wide range. At the level of the mind, for example, they include the ability to respond to and focus creative inspiration, as well as skills in objective perception, integrity and ethics, and understanding the needs of others. At the emotional level, the expression of light requires the ability to use goodwill correctly to nurture ideals, plus an ability to control negativity. Physically, the intention to express light requires skills in productivity, innovation, and helpfulness.

Finally, education is the process which enables us to fulfill our obligation to focus light more purposefully and abundantly. While light is already universal, it only becomes individualized as we learn to focus it in meaningful ways through the finite conditions of our life. We do not become an agent of love, wisdom, and courage merely by worshiping these ideals in the abstract; we must learn to focus them in our own life. The lessons to be mastered may be as simple as cultivating a healthy self-image—or as complex as the work of white magic.

To be effective, education should be oriented to the development of consciousness, not the accumulation of facts and techniques. Too often, unfortunately, education is viewed in terms of the transmission of knowledge—for example, the instruction of students in the rules and facts of mathematics. While a knowledge of rules and facts is important and should not be overlooked, the *emphasis* of education should always be on helping students learn to think—for instance, to think mathematically. To some degree, of course, students do learn to think mathematically as a result of studying facts and rules—but not nearly as much as many educators imagine.

Learning should therefore be regarded as a multifaceted science itself. We must learn how to learn—how to study, discern facts, intuit their deeper meanings and applications, fit them into larger patterns, and relate them to the design of life. This is not a casual enterprise; it should be accorded a proper measure of respect and priority.

As this idea applies to our growth as an agent of light, it is important to keep in mind that we are not just trying to collect a large portfolio of esoteric ideas. The knowledge of ideas does not make us wise nor bring us light; knowing what to do with good ideas does. The real value of an idea is always in its application. To make the most of our learning experiences, therefore, we must pursue a subject until we understand it so thoroughly that we can apply its inner wisdom in helpful and meaningful ways in our own life. Several corollaries for spiritual growth are suggested by this precept:

• Little is gained by a lifetime of flitting from one esoteric discipline to another, without mastering any of them. Because it is the process of "drawing forth" the light of spirit, education requires us to focus our efforts and time on worthwhile lessons, and pursue them until we are thoroughly proficient in them.

• The student should view himself as the "co-teacher."

Learning proceeds most quickly when approached in a cooperative spirit. Our true teacher is the light within us. The role of physical teachers is to remind us of this fact, help guide us toward this inner light, and encourage us to continue learning even when we are discouraged and ready to quit.

• The teacher needs to view himself as a "master learner." His role is not so much to impart knowledge, because true knowledge is discovered in the light of the soul, but to demonstrate what learning is. He should be a role model for other learners to emulate, by conveying to his students his love of wisdom and the dignity of a well-trained mind.

• Our goal in learning should always be to acquire a better understanding of light. Lessons in aggressive behavior, competitiveness, manipulation, and creative paranoia are not worth learning.

• To be a good learner, we must love and revere the potential of the noble human mind. There are too many people who actually try to undermine the value of a well-trained, enlightened mind; they are threatened by intelligence, genius, and talent. These range from anti-intellectuals on the one hand, who are simply embarrassed by anyone who exposes their ignorance, to fascists of the mind on the other hand, who attempt to limit and reduce freedom of thought and self-expression, directly or indirectly. Part of being an inspired learner is to see the damage done by these attitudes, and to honor the mind and revere the brilliance of the inner light.

• At times, learning new lessons requires the unlearning of old habits, limited ideas, and prejudices. The true learner constantly examines his attitudes and established beliefs, to see what constitutes barriers to further learning. He then removes them.

• Every circumstance and condition of life can be an opportunity to learn, because each gives us a new chance to focus more light into our understanding, behavior, and talents. But the primary purpose of the events of life is not to teach us lessons; it is to provide conditions which will allow us to make useful and helpful contributions. Education is intended to be the servant of the inner light as it seeks to train the personality to cooperate with it in its creative endeavors. It is not an end unto itself. Once we have "drawn forth" the light of our spirit, *we are expected to do something enlightened with it!*

We should therefore make it a high priority to learn about learning. At first, this may seem a bit simplistic. But our cultural conditioning regarding the goals and nature of education has become so perverse that it is important for each intelligent person to pause and reexamine the purposes of learning—and what he or she is doing to support and nourish it.

Before we begin, however, it is important to recognize that we do have a source of wisdom—our inner light—which can answer our questions and guide us to a proper understanding of the learning process. We do not really learn much by brooding over our difficulties or compiling a list of grievances; we learn by invoking the light, so that we may understand them.

In this spirit, then, we should thoroughly review the important lessons of our life. What kind of lessons enabled us to acquire our most important skills and understanding? Which lessons have enriched our character? How well have we cooperated with the learning process? Have the lessons been fully learned—or is there more to be mastered?

In considering questions of this nature, we should pursue our insights to deeper levels. If one of the lessons we have learned, for example, is efficiency, what caused us to learn it? Did we read about it in a textbook and decide it was the optimum way of living? Or did we experience a series of events which subtly instructed us in the value of efficient behavior? How could we have cooperated more effectively with these lessons and speeded our learning?

By answering these questions, we become more aware of how we learn the lessons of being an agent of light. Then, with this understanding in mind, we can turn our attention to the present and ask ourself:

"If I am to fulfill my work as an agent of light, what more do I need to learn? How best can I learn it?"

These two questions should be applied to every aspect of life. We should ask, for example, what we need to learn about our attitudes, responsibilities, and performance at work; what we need to learn about expressing goodwill, compassion, cooperation, and tact; what we need to learn about self-discipline, right speech, and overreacting; and what we need to learn about the mind and its uses, creativity, and the soul. There are, of course, many other facets of life which ought to be explored as well.

As we pursue the answers to these questions, we should understand that the light provides more than ideas and facts. Light is composed of wisdom and power. It is living force. As we seek its tutelage, therefore, we receive more than instruction alone; we are touched by the impulse to grow itself. If we are open to this impulse, it can transform the way we live. It can enlighten us.

We are expected to harness and embrace the impulse to grow. This is the obligation of every human being. Harnessing this impulse is not especially difficult; it can begin with this simple exercise. But it should be viewed as a lifelong commitment—an investment in our destiny.

Of all spiritual assets, the greatest is our capacity to grow. If we ignore this asset, we may well find ourself bankrupt. But if we properly invest it in our daily activities, it will increase and become a rich endowment.

2.

How Learning Occurs

One of the great problems of modern education is the widespread failure to truly understand how learning occurs. There are few countries in the world today that do not provide an opportunity for their young to attend school, acquire knowledge, and, if suited for it, go on to higher education. And yet, the overwhelming percentage of people who take advantage of this educational opportunity leave their last class knowing very little more about *how to learn* than when they first matriculated. They may have absorbed an immense quantity of facts, statistics, theories, opinions, and related knowledge. They may have also acquired a variety of technical skills—in writing, speaking, logic, science, engineering, the arts, or music. But unless they have experimented on their own, or been fortunate enough to study with an inspired teacher, they have not learned how to learn—or even to respect the value of pursuing knowledge. They do not know how to continue learning once they leave the halls of academia behind.

This is unfortunate, because education is supposed to be something more than a process of absorbing knowledge and memorizing formulas. Each level of education is meant to *expand* the student's capacity to perceive life clearly, understand its meaning, and contribute to society. As a result, each phase of education should be a journey of self-awareness, discovery, and creativity—a journey the student continues to pursue after formal education is completed.

All too often, however, it is not. Our standard concepts of learning put the major emphasis on the knowledge and skills to be learned, not on the potential of the one who is learning to use them. As a result, the student never really becomes involved in the learning process. The formulas, dates, theories, speculations, and facts we are expected to learn are always something *external* to ourself—something we learn to manipulate and use, but never assimilate. History, for instance, remains a body of information about mankind's past, not a potential source of intelligent insight into the patterns and cycles which govern our own individual life as well as the whole of humanity. The study of literature is treated as a series of exercises in formulating opinions and defending them, instead of an introduction to the power of the personal myth in defining who we are and what we are doing here. And science becomes a dry analysis of observable physical phenomena, instead of a quest for greater understanding of the intelligence that pervades all of life, including ourself.

Nowhere is this problem more obvious than in the areas of psychology and personal growth, where the focus of learning is directed almost entirely to making changes in outer behavior instead of enriching our character. We may learn through self-hypnosis or behavior modification to suppress a bad habit such as a nasty temper, but have we learned anything which will help us solve other problems of personal growth? Have we learned anything which will help us when the suppressed anger finally resurfaces?

No. We have learned some tricks which may or may not help us in the short term, but we have neither added to our virtue nor refined our consciousness in any fundamental way. Our learning has therefore been limited and incomplete; it has kept us trapped in mundane patterns of living and understanding. It has failed to do what education ought to do.

Education ought to enable us to break through our limitations and expand both our skills and our awareness to a higher degree of competence. And when it does not, there is serious doubt as to whether any real learning is occurring.

To understand how learning occurs, we must redefine the role of the intelligent person in pursuing an education. In modern education, the mind is taught and encouraged to *respond* to knowledge—to gather, memorize, and process facts and other data. It is thought that learning occurs as the mind becomes more and more skilled in *reflecting* the light of what is known. The mind, however, is an instrument of consciousness, and therefore is a product of light itself. In addition to reflecting the light of what is known, the human mind has the capacity to explore the nature of light, cast its own light, and become a creative agent of light. The role of learning should consequently do more than just train the mind to gather, memorize, and process data. It should teach the mind to discover its own rich heritage in the light and harness the relationship between its own light and the light of what is known. Learning occurs as the mind absorbs and radiates the light of ideas.

A simple example may help illustrate this point. The mind that has learned to reflect the light of what is known is able to take a recipe developed by a master chef, teach itself the culinary skills it needs to perform the various steps in the recipe, and then use it to cook a delicious meal. In this way, the knowledge of the chef has become available to this person. But a mind that has learned to be creative is able to take the same recipe and tap the light of its inspiration. Such a person can not only cook the meal described in the recipe, but also use its inspiration to generate many other recipes and cooking techniques.

Learning is meant to be an event in consciousness, not just in outer behavior or form. It is measured not in terms of our ability to recall facts and figures but in terms of how much inner change is occurring in our *capacity to know—and to use what we know.*

This principle is important to anyone who wants to learn, but especially to the agent of light. Standard methods of learning are often quite inadequate for the task of becoming an effective representative of the inner life. They are oriented toward the acquisition of finite facts and skills—not the growth of consciousness. Many people who embark on the spiritual path, for example, plunge themselves into the study of esoteric knowledge and lore, learning all about rounds and chains. They become drunk on knowledge, yet often all they have done is expand their memory. They have not increased their understanding of how divine life operates in their life, and what it means to act creatively as an agent of light.

The same problem frequently arises in a different context, too. An aspirant will read a profound book describing some aspect of the life of spirit and see the value of these ideas in his or her own life. Yet two or three weeks later, the individual will be embroiled again in old conflicts, unable to utilize the profound principles that had been so inspiring. Why is this so? Because the mind is being used only to reflect the light of these ideas, not work creatively with them to change the actual structure of consciousness.

There are many educational experts who will flatly declare that they cannot teach self-awareness, comprehension, or creativity; all they can do is present facts and let each individual struggle with them. But this is not true. Learning does not occur by wading into a swamp of statistics and facts and hoping to find solid ground; it occurs as we pursue the light within ideas.

Learning is a highly individualistic process. A group of students can learn the same lessons together, but the comprehension of each individual will be determined by his or her capacity to learn. Simply put, the degree to which we can discover and learn about anything depends on how much we have discovered and learned about ourself. The greater our self-awareness, the more we can accelerate the learning process.

To do this, we must break away from those who would "get in touch with their feelings," and learn instead to "get in touch with our mind." We must involve ourself in the learning process and become aware of our personal *learning mechanism*—the structure in consciousness in which learning occurs. There are several points to examine:

• How do we perceive our world? Are we skilled at examining life as it is, or do we tend to perceive events, people, and data with a highly personal bias? Do we try to understand ideas and phenomena which are complex and mysterious, or do we demand simplistic solutions and comforting explanations? Many people have mental blocks against entertaining certain types of ideas. The most common examples would be the fear of confronting such ideas as death, the inner dimensions of life, and God. Such blocks paralyze the learning process, until they are removed.

• How do we analyze events and draw conclusions? Do we treat the facts of a situation superficially, or do we try to put them in a larger context that includes various perspectives, trends leading up to the event, and the probable outcomes? Unless we draw conclusions based on the fullest information available, learning will degenerate into the mere validation of our previous beliefs.

• What interests us? Why do we focus on these aspects of life and not on others? Are we interested in these things because we want to learn more about them—or are they just entertaining or titillating?

• What do we militantly ignore? Both individuals and

scoiety regard certain ideas as "off limits" to discussion or exploration. As a result, it becomes almost impossible to learn anything of value about them.

• What motivates us to learn? Do we learn in order to show off our knowledge? Or is our motivation defensive— we learn so no one else will get an advantage over us? Some people learn as a way of compensating for a poor self-image; others learn in order to get a better paying job. The nature of our motivation will determine to a large degree how effectively we do learn. If our reason for learning is to show off or earn money, our learning will be superficial. But if we learn in order to better understand ourself and make better use of our mind, our progress will be real and worthwhile.

• Do we initiate the learning process and consider it our obligation to learn? Or do we wait for others to teach us? Are we able to discover the lessons involved in life's experiences, or are we still dependent upon the tutelage of others?

The value of such introspection is that it helps us become aware of the state of our learning mechanism. We can always acquire facts without changing the inner structure of our consciousness. But, if we are learning the lessons of light, each one will expand our learning mechanism. It will refocus our values, transform our attitudes, reshape our views, and improve our methodologies.

When we have acquired some knowledge of ourself, and how we learn, then it becomes possible to use the light we have discovered in our own mind to become aware of the meaning and creative potential of ideas, skills, circumstances, relationships, and all the phenomena of life. But even at this stage, we must be careful not to become just a collector of facts and data. We should seek not just to observe and examine the conditions of life, but to observe and examine *the light within* these conditions.

To do this, we must be willing to:

1. Accept the world *as it is.* All too many people, even scientists, try to deal with life as they have conceptualized it to be, rather than as it is. As a result, they seek mainly to verify their assumptions, not learn anything new about life.

2. Investigate *every facet* of the facts and phenomena we are examining, not just those which are the easiest to uncover or the most appealing.

3. Consider the *fullness* of the phenomena of life, not just their superficial appearance in the physical plane. In other words, we must be willing to look at the inner side of life—the hidden motives and fears of people, the inner essence of ideas, the pattern of human events, the meaning of our experiences, and so on. Unless we are willing to do this, it will not be possible to work with the light within these phenomena, which is the basis of real learning.

For true learning to occur, therefore, we must train the mind to look for and understand:

• The principles governing the situation of life we are examining, not just "the facts." We know a lot about the facts surrounding the formation of this country, for example, but very little about the principles which provided the momentum for it, and whether or not they are still being honored by the way society is structured in modern America.

35

• The antecedents of events, not just the events themselves. Whether in science, history, or human development, events do not happen in isolation or at random. They have antecedents which, if carefully traced, usually reveal a larger pattern of order and intelligence that must be considered in order to comprehend the meaning of the single event. This larger pattern is often the key to the light within the situation.

• The implications of the facts we have gathered (both from outer and inner observation), not just opinions. The growth of modern psychology has been hampered, for example, by the habit of psychologists to use the opinions and reactions of people as the basis for their theories, rather than the implications of the actual design of human consciousness.

• Insights into the meaning of facts, not just superficial judgments. There are three levels to any idea or pattern—its outer appearance, its inner meaning, and the power of its self-expression. It is easy to make judgments based on outer appearance, but this seldom leads to genuine learning. We must seek instead to penetrate to the inner levels of meaning and power, where we can tap true insight.

• The consequences of proposed uses of our ideas, not just current need. Before embarking on any experiment for the purpose of learning, we should carefully examine the consequences of pursuing this particular course of action, and be sure it will lead to a sound learning experience. All too many "experiments" in learning end up producing results other than what was intended.

• The relationship of the specific to the whole. It is easy

to get caught up in the seeming uniqueness of problems and ideas, but this prevents us from tapping the light within the form. The habit of looking for the larger picture into which specific conditions fit greatly accelerates the learning process.

• Causes and motivations, not just assumptions. The orientation toward facts and figures keeps many people trapped in the level of learning about *what* happens. They fail to comprehend *why* and *how* things happen. Yet we can only work creatively with the light within events and ideas if we understand *why* they are constituted as they are and *how* they are designed to function best.

• The potential for transformation, not just mere repetition. Whether we are dealing with human behavior, ideas, or scientific discoveries, the light within these phenomena has a potential to expand and be enriched. One of the great keys to learning is our own ability to assist in the enlightened transformation of whatever it is we are studying. Involving ourself in the growth process in this way stimulates every facet of our own learning, and helps us become truly creative.

• How we can integrate what we are learning into our own values, attitudes, and behavior. Learning does not occur by "adding on" new facts and skills; it occurs by restructuring the way in which we express the light within us. In this way, the learning process comes full circle; having begun with the need to expand our self-awareness, it reaches completion by lifting our self-awareness to a higher level. The learning mechanism itself benefits and grows.

Indeed, the true test that learning is occurring is not our

ability to recite facts and statistics, but our ability to take new skills and insights and apply them to a wide range of problems. This is the sign that what we have learned has become a permanent part of our consciousness, not just something we know for a while and then forget.

There are many ways we can become a more conscious participant in the learning process. One of the most powerful is to choose a single area of personal responsibility and see how much genuine learning can be achieved.

Our examination might begin by asking ourself:

How have I defined my responsibility? In terms of physical duties alone? Or in terms of the principles it embodies, the inner design for fulfilling this responsibility, and why this is important to my life?

Have I viewed this responsibility as an opportunity to learn and grow as a person? How have I perceived this responsibility in the past? How have I defined my obligations? What motivates me to fulfill this responsibility or learn more about performing it intelligently?

As these questions bring useful new insights, others can be examined:

Into what larger patterns does this responsibility fit? How do I relate to these larger patterns? In what ways do I need to grow? What skills and human qualities must I develop to do so? In what ways do I need to transform my values, habits, and character?

The effort to learn the skills and new understanding needed to fulfill this one responsibility more wisely will not only stimulate our progress in this area of living, but also help us grow more rapidly in the way we handle all responsibilities.

It will also teach us a great deal about the way learning occurs.

3.

The Need For Unlearning

To be effective, each new lesson in personal and spiritual growth must challenge a skill, concept, or belief we have held before. Most of us seem to assume that we can leave the empty husks of our earlier knowledge behind, like so many peanut shells, and they will eventually dissolve. But this is not actually true. Unless we take active steps to "unlearn" that which we have learned—but no longer need—it will remain in our subconscious as a seed that can sprout forth again at some later date.

This is just common sense. Children do not continue to wear baby clothes after they have outgrown them. Nor do we see many thirty-year-olds sucking on pacifiers. By the time we have become adults, we have packed away our toys and games.

As we confront each new challenge of adult life, we are

meant to do the same thing: trade in old ideas, methodologies, concepts, and beliefs for new, more effective and enlightening ones. But we do not just "add on" something new and better. The process of learning involves an exchange: we are meant to trade in our old ways of thinking and behaving for new ideas, insights, and revelations.

In other words, we must unlearn what we have learned some time in the past, replacing it with what we are learning now. If we fail to do so, the old, outdated ideas, beliefs, and procedures will remain in our subconscious, subtly warring with our new ideas and undermining the firmness of our resolve. We become hesitant and uncertain of how to proceed, trapped in a completely unnecessary ambivalence.

It is therefore important to pause regularly in our efforts to grow and learn, in order to assess the lessons from our past that we now need to unlearn. Some of the more notorious traps to look for include:

• Accepting ideas because they are popular. It is easy to believe that certain ideas and concepts are right, just because all of our friends—and society—accept them. For this reason, popular thought and established traditions often go unchallenged, even though they may be silly or harmful. In today's society, for example, it is common to believe that it is healthy to express anger. Yet there is ample scientific evidence that anger damages the health of the physical body.

• Preferring simple generalizations as explanations for the complexities of life. The carefree attitudes of adolescence, for example, must be traded in before a person will be ready for the adult commitments of marriage and

41

parenting. Just so, we cannot rely wholly on "what our bodies tell us" as we seek to understand the complex problems of personal health.

• Difficulty in admitting error. Some people are so absorbed in protecting their ego strength that they cannot admit when they have erred. They therefore compound mistakes by defending self-serving deceptions that need to be updated.

• Maintaining the status quo. Many people find it much easier to keep things the same than to risk the uncertainty of change—or growth. Many would rather know in part than to risk the implications of knowing something in its fullness. The classic example of this is the person who "controls" his anxiety by avoiding all potential threats—rather than learning to heal the anxiety itself.

• Comforting theories that bear no relationship to the real world. We often let theories seduce us into thinking in clichés and stereotypes. A hostile fundamentalist, for example, may find comfort in the belief that God will punish all sinners, whereas an arrogant rationalist would take refuge in the notion that there is no divine order or law.

• Fanatic obsessions. Some people adhere fanatically to certain notions, putting so much emphasis on them that they become twisted and distorted beyond recognition. Gradually, their lives become consumed with finding fault with everyone who challenges them, until it becomes impossible to see the real world and the role they are meant to play in it. An example would be the perfectionist who insists on knowing every variable in advance, and is therefore rarely able to get started on projects.

• Limited perceptions. If we consider only physical phenomena, we will limit our understanding of life considerably. If we think only in terms of immediate consequences, we cannot take advantage of long-term developments. If we listen only to people who represent our point of view, we severely restrict our ability to comprehend life. These problems thwart growth in business and government, as well as individually.

• Relativism. Many of us sabotage growth by imposing our subjective, personalized viewpoint on all new experiences. We explain events in terms of how we feel about them, rather than in terms of their inherent meaning. As a result, we trap ourself in superstition and "magical thinking."

For the agent of light, these various traps all relate to one common challenge: the need to shift the focus of our thought and action from the personality to the soul. With each new lesson in life that is presented to us, we need to identify skills, habits, and beliefs of the personality that now conflict with the new talent, pattern, or wisdom that is emerging. These old patterns, of course, are actually the sum of everything the personality "knows" about this aspect of life that contradicts the wisdom and guidance of the higher self.

The exact lessons that must be unlearned vary, of course, from individual to individual. But a number of lessons stand out, because they remain unlearned in so many people. They constitute the primary body of knowledge and skill that must be removed from our subconscious if we are to

43

be free enough to grow. The major categories of these lessons are:

• Facts and assumptions. We assume, usually for no reason whatever, that our experiences—and our interpretations of them—are valid and correct. In other words, if we remember being threatened physically by our father as a child, we assume that a) our memory is correct and b) the anger we feel toward our father today is legitimate. Yet both of these assumptions may be wrong. It is easy for children to misconstrue the meaning of actions their parents take. It is also silly to express anger over something that happened thirty years ago.

Another way in which we stumble over facts and assumptions is through stereotyping. It has become popular for minorities to label all white people racists, not because of what they believe, but because of the limitations of growing up in a cultural environment that did not present a minority perspective. This kind of inverse bigotry destroys any effort to tap into the guidance of the higher self and deal with people as they are, not as someone else perceives them.

• Attitudes and beliefs. One of the strongest forces which impedes learning is arrogance—the "I know it all, don't bother me with reality" syndrome. It is important to keep our knowledge open-ended, and always be willing to revise beliefs as life shows us our shortcomings.

An habitually cynical attitude can block off the impulse to grow in much the same way. If we become convinced that life is not evolving, we may well become indifferent, uncaring. Such a thoughtform can become an obstacle that

44

cannot be penetrated. Just so, angry defensiveness, what used to be known as a "chip on the shoulder," can also obstruct meaningful growth. We become so absorbed in protecting ourself against the onslaught of life that we become unable to pursue new avenues of opportunity.

• Ingrained character traits. Many of us take pride in our individuality, but in some cases this pride is not well-founded. Many of the character traits we take such care to preserve are negative, harmful ones that keep us from growing. Pettiness and smallmindedness, for example, are mental habits that keep us focused in unimportant details, while we miss the larger picture. These character traits make it almost impossible to develop abstract thinking skills—until they are unlearned.

Rebelliousness can poison us in much the same way. We often need to reject the false authority of demagogues, but rebelliousness too easily pits us against all authority—including the direction of our higher self. When it does, we soon become trapped in the mesh of our own rebellion.

Mental laziness is another trait that many people need to unlearn. Throughout our schooling, many of us have been taught to absorb facts without examining them and to accept interpretations without questioning them. To properly develop the mind, these patterns of laziness must be overcome, and replaced by more active, discerning habits.

• Injurious self-concepts. An alarming number of people today suffer from a "victim consciousness"—the belief that they have been irreparably damaged and harmed by their parents, a spouse, the church, or society. This justifies their suffering, but also traps them in a level they cannot out-grow—until they learn to stop being a victim.

At a more global level, the concept of nihilism has much the same impact. If we believe that life is meaningless, then there is no point in trying to grow and evolve. Such a belief amounts to a direct rejection of the higher self.

• Conventional wisdom. There is a whole host of fads, beliefs, and concepts that are accepted by most people without question. Much of what is presently being labeled "politically correct" falls into this category—a consensus of thought that has been accepted just because a group of people have chosen to believe it. The idea that poverty causes crime is an example of conventional wisdom. It flies in the face of all spiritual wisdom, but is nonetheless almost universally accepted as true. Before society will actually be able to reduce crime, this simplistic notion will have to be unlearned.

Our ideas about money, sex, and power are all highly constricted by conventional wisdom—and further discussion is prohibited by taboo. The way we measure success (and define failure) is usually at the most superficial level—far different than the way the higher self would define it.

Traditions are a stunning example of the need to un-learn established knowledge. A tradition is formed as society tries to institutionalize a good idea. But good ideas need to be updated frequently to remain valid. A well-established tradition will actually impede this updating process, rather than assist it. In our society, for example, it is traditional to work until sixty-five. As our life expectancy increases, however, it may make sense to prolong careers to seventy or even seventy-five. But no matter how logical and reasonable a change like this may be, tradition will fight—and delay it.

The art of unlearning is primarily a question of shifting our awareness from these traps to a more inclusive perspective. We are not denying what we have known in the past, or in any way repressing it. Instead, we are putting it in a larger context that alters its meaning. At the same time, we are integrating new insight or information into our character.

The actual process of unlearning consists of five steps:

1. Admitting our limits and challenging our assumptions. In order to do this, we have to break through our arrogance and belief that we know it all, or at least most of it. We need to take a large dose of humility and realize that the world is vast and exciting—and there is an unlimited measure of what we can still learn. As we cultivate a proper level of humility, we then need to reflect upon the fact that some of the ideas, beliefs, and habits we have defended so fiercely in the past have been wrong and ought to be updated, revised—and even discarded.

2. Purging shallow thinking. Many of the limitations we need to unlearn are inherent within the simplistic processes we mistakenly call "thinking." We "think" dualistically, separating life into black and white, good and evil, all or none, and them or us categories. We generalize on the basis of scanty evidence, leaping to unfounded conclusions. We act on theories without validating them. As a result, we cripple our mental faculties. In order to reverse this

tendency, we need to become more attentive to the actual facts of life. Instead of filtering our perceptions through a screen of personal assumptions, we must learn to give more weight to our actual experiences. We need to listen to what life is teaching us, rather than what we want to hear—or even what we expect. This process will enable us to reject ideas and theories not helpful to us.

3. Restoring rationality to the thinking process. We are not meant to be ruled by our emotions or attitudes; on the contrary, we are meant to develop a perspective on life which lets us adjust our feelings as the situation demands. If we need to be calm, it is silly to let our emotions dominate us with irritability. If we need to cooperate in order to preserve a relationship, it is foolish to let ourself become angry. We therefore need to learn to set aside automatic emotional reactions such as irritation, fear, worry, and anger—not just because they are harmful, which they are, but because they undermine our potential for expressing enthusiasm, curiosity, hope, and goodwill as well. We must learn to base our attitudes on enlightened values, rather than the explosive feelings or rebellious mood of the moment.

These attitudes cannot be changed, in most cases, just by willing that it be done. Instead, we must carefully and patiently train the emotions to respond to and express the goodwill, joy, and patience of the higher self. Most importantly, we must define for ourself what is a mature, intelligent expression of the emotions.

4. Developing a healthy and inclusive self-concept. Instead of believing that we are God's greatest gift to human-

ity, or a pitiful wretch who deserves all the misery and humiliation that fills our life, we need to understand that we have a rich potential for growth, love, and wisdom that continues to exist regardless of who we have been and how we have acted in the past. Like every human being, we bring with us a divine endowment we are meant to discover and use. If we identify too much with unpleasant memories and old patterns of victimization, we may forget about this divine endowment. Even worse, we will close ourself to many learning experiences and ideas. Life is larger than a few bad experiences; to the degree that we have let discouragement or resentment cripple us, we need to unlearn these harmful lessons and get back to cultivating our noble potential.

5. Loving to learn. The cycle of unlearning will only be complete if we cultivate an ongoing passion for learning, so that our growth becomes self-initiated. Most people learn the lessons of life only reluctantly, when forced. And once acquired, we tend to defend them, whether or not they are still helpful. Instead of being afraid that growth will expose our weaknesses, we should revel in the opportunities that come to us to learn something new, overcome limitations, and unlearn whatever has trapped us.

Learning should be a joyous experience—and unless the process of unlearning is, too, it will be short-circuited.

To determine what we need to unlearn, we need to examine where the learning process has become bogged down. In what areas of life have we become unable to express joy? This is a certain sign that something needs to be unlearned.

The first step is to decide which idea, belief, habit, or convention needs to be unlearned. The answer may be perfectly obvious—or may take months to comprehend. Whatever it is, it will probably fit one of the categories described earlier.

Once the lesson to be unlearned has been identified, the next step is to decide what needs to be removed, adjusted, or added. An arrogant attitude, for example, would have to be removed and replaced with a more reverent, humble one. A poor self-image would need to be replaced by a stronger conviction that there is a reservoir of noble potential deep within us that we can tap.

Whatever changes need to be made, we need to rehearse them thoroughly at the level of our creative imagination. If we have a hard time thinking of ourself in an ideal way, then we can work mentally with a role model that illustrates the right way. We must continue rehearsing the changes to be made until we are thoroughly confident in our ability to act in these updated, improved ways. We should then incorporate these new patterns of thinking and acting into our daily self-expression.

As we work in this way, it is important to invoke the guidance and support of the higher self. This enables spirit to add its joy and blessing to the changes we are making.

4.

The Meaning of Our Experiences

Learning is a process that depends almost entirely on the student. Even the greatest teacher cannot force a student to learn if the pupil is unwilling. Nor can the greatest teacher prevent careless students from misunderstanding the lesson being taught, turning wisdom into opinion and truth into propaganda. It would be just as preposterous to believe that the *Encyclopedia Britannica* is somehow responsible for the shallow and unperceptive conclusions drawn by those readers who insist on reading the words on the pages through the narrowmindedness of bias and prejudice.

It is said that experience is a great teacher—and it often is. But just because the experiences of life can teach us wonderful truths does not in any way guarantee that we will learn from them—or even learn the right lesson. After all, many of the experiences of life are painful or tragic—the loss of a loved one, dismissal at work, or a long, painful illness. If we react to these events by becoming bitter or insulted, then we have probably learned the wrong lesson. If we respond to the lessons of life by trying to dodge them and avoid our responsibilities, then who can we fault—except ourself? If we greet every difficulty and inconvenience with a barrage of complaints, how can we expect truth and wisdom to get through to us? If we collapse in exhaustion and defeat every time we confront a seemingly immovable obstacle, how can we expect to achieve anything? Events may be trying to teach us, but we are not cooperating. We are learning the wrong lessons.

Actually, experience is more of a great textbook about life than a great teacher. Life presents us with a series of lessons—but the learning of them is not automatic. It is up to us. If we are lazy, we will miss the message of life's lessons. If we are biased and closed-minded, we will distort the meaning of what we are experiencing. If we are stubborn, we will repeat our errors. If we are selfish, we will foolishly compound our mistakes, by trying to get an advantage over others.

To learn from our experiences, therefore, we need to develop some proper study habits. Above all, we will have to learn that just experiencing life does not necessarily teach us anything at all—or at least anything useful. For experiences to become lessons in life, we must be able to digest their meaning. We must be able to extract from the pain or pleasure of the actual event the kernel of wisdom or insight that can help us grow as a human being, mentally, emotionally, physically, and spiritually.

Once we have learned this basic skill, then the events and problems of life become an invaluable resource for learning and growing. But until we seize control of this process, the events and experiences of life will probably remain nothing more than a source of confusion and bewilderment as we blindly try to pursue pleasure and avoid pain.

The word "experience" gives us a big clue to the art of learning directly from life. An experience is not just a physical event, an episode of life that happens to us. An event becomes an experience as we interact, respond, and learn from it. We do not necessarily have any choice in what events happen to us. Surely no one deliberately chooses to be sideswiped by another automobile at sixty miles an hour, yet such events do occur. When they do, however, we have a wide range of choice in deciding how we will respond to the accident—or any other event in life. We can respond wisely and maturely—or selfishly and immaturely. We can respond angrily and defensively—or compassionately and thoughtfully. How we respond determines how much—or how little—we will learn from this event.

Suppose a friend reneges on a commitment. If we feel betrayed and unable to forgive our friend, this type of reactiveness would indicate that we are not learning from this experience. On the other hand, if we endeavor to understand the motive of our friend in making this decision, and try to understand the pressures he or she was facing, we may be able to see this action in an entirely new light. We may be able not only to forgive, but also learn to handle such disappointments sensibly. Consequently, the actions our friend took become partly helpful rather than entirely harmful to us.

The event is the same, regardless of our response. But as our reactions change, a confusing experience can become a meaningful lesson. We, of course, are the one who has added the meaning, by searching for it.

We are the factor that determines what we will learn from life. If we harness this innate potential, there is no limit to what we can learn. But we cannot wait for it to be forced upon us. We must make the first move and take the initiative to grow in character and competence. Indeed, too many adults stop growing in early adulthood; they rely on automatic subconscious responses to life. No matter what happens to them, their response is a monotony of reactiveness:

- They complain. They know something is amiss, but expect someone else to fix it.
- They blame. They know something is wrong, but refuse to take any responsibility for it.
- They get angry. They take umbrage at the fact that nothing has been done to resolve this problem.
- They become defensive. Whatever is wrong, it is not their fault.
- They try to avoid the problem in the future, by running away from it in the present.

The second great step in learning from experience, therefore, is to identify and dispel our own personal resistance. Instead of viewing life's events as threats and hardships to be avoided at all costs, we can view them as a textbook of lessons in spiritual growth. We should learn to value the wisdom and maturity we can gain from our experiences, even painful ones, and teach ourself how to appreciate these events, instead of regretting them, fearing them, or blaming others for them.

In specific, we must confront our personal resistance head on and deflate it. This is done by replacing our apathy, griping, defeatism, and scapegoating with a new and better set of alternatives:

• The desire to learn. We need to be willing to accept the events of life as they come to us and learn as much as we can from them. Although others may view an event as a tragedy or an embarrassment, we approach it from a different perspective—learning something of value even from suffering or discomfort.

• Curiosity. As we start to pay attention to the lessons the textbook of life can teach us, we begin to sense how vast and unlimited these lessons can be. We therefore need to sharpen our curiosity to learn as much about the workings of life as we can. We do not need to be able to read dusty manuscripts in ancient Senzar to learn about divine law, after all. We simply need to be able to see how divine law governs and directs our own life—and the lives of others around us—by observing what works and does not work, over a long period of time.

• Wisdom. We begin to view the world as a benevolent place that helps all of creation grow toward its perfection. The events of life are neither capricious strokes of good fortune nor punishments, but opportunities to take the next step forward on our path of evolution. When seen with inner wisdom, these events and the sequence in which they occur make sense. They are confusing only to people who do not make the effort to comprehend them.

We must therefore leave our childishness behind us and become an adult. Growing up is, after all, a process of overcoming resistance while adding maturity to our self-expression. The adult learns that mastery of life does not come by attacking it, but by learning to cooperate with it. We must therefore abandon our adversarial attitudes toward life—"us versus them"—and learn to act in harmony with whatever life is trying to teach us. We must cooperate with experience, drinking fully of the fountain of life, not recoiling negatively from it.

Most people, unfortunately, do not have this gusto for learning. When confronted with difficulties and opportunities to grow, they retreat instead into the comforting illusions of their wish life—of what they want to believe. They create an artificial world that pleases and consoles them, instead of dealing honestly with the real issues of their life.

Naturally, this type of self-deception can only be sustained for a while. Sooner or later, the events of life will expose these illusions for what they are. At this point, we may feel disappointment or outrage, and continue to avoid the real problem. But eventually we realize the foolishness of this reaction and the emptiness of our approach to life. We will be ready to grow.

The struggle, then, tends to be between our fanciful interpretation of life (our wish life) and the harsh reality of what happens to us (the facts of life). The experiences of life will continue to chip away at the façade of our wish life until we stop playing these make-believe games. For this reason, the textbook of our experiences is especially helpful in assisting us to learn:

• How we are controlled by emotional hot spots. If we are quick to flare up in anger, the textbook of life will underscore this problem for us, as we repeatedly lose our temper over insignificant events. If we have trapped ourself in worry, the textbook of life will also reveal this problem, by constantly presenting us with issues to worry about. By observing the patterns of our emotional reactions to the events of life, we can discover where we are weak—and recognize the need for more mature alternatives.

• How we have made errors in judgment and acted on false assumptions. Those materialistic skeptics who arbitrarily reject the benevolence of life and the healing power of spirit, for example, may well find themselves stricken with a disease that cannot be cured by medical treatments. In desperation, they may be forced to explore the possibilities of being healed by prayer and other spiritual methods, thereby breaking down the limits of their bigotry.

• Limitations of skill and competence. Many people suffer from too much confidence and too little talent and skill. Parents who believe, for instance, that they know *exactly* what is right for their children—and do not heed the suggestions of others—may soon learn from life to be more humble.

• Limitations of courage and perseverance. There is only one effective way we can learn to trust in the life and wisdom of the soul, and that is to go through experiences which virtually exhaust our personal strength and courage, leaving only the power of the higher self to rescue us. When we can recognize and rely on this inner strength, we have learned a truly valuable lesson.

• Limitations of self-awareness. We are frequently hampered by blind spots and self-deception. Spiritual aspirants, for example, often believe they are far more detached from the materialistic forces of life than they actually are. The experiences of life repeatedly remind us that even as we become progressively more aware of the soul, our daily thoughts, feelings, and acts are still primarily shaped by outer events and our perceptions of them. In other words, we are largely materialistic.

There is no guarantee that we will learn any of these lessons. But if we falter, we will find that the textbook of life will repeat itself—a specific lesson will continue to recur until we awaken to the realization that we must change.

Life is always intelligent and lawful, even if it sometimes seems capricious and pointless. We always have the option to refuse to grow, by turning our backs on the lessons of our experiences. But even then life is determined to help us grow. It will work relentlessly to encourage us to overcome our resistance, assume our responsibilities, and seize the abundant opportunities for growth that come to us.

In discussing the textbook of our experiences, it is important to understand that we are meant to derive more than just new insights from the lessons of life. We are meant to acquire new capacities and skills in self-expression. If the lesson to be learned is tolerance, for example, it is not enough just to become sensitive and sympathetic. We must learn to embrace others with goodwill and patience.

Nevertheless, the first step in learning from the events of life usually begins with understanding them. As we review any event or experience, current or past, we need to ask ourself questions that will help us put this episode of life in a proper perspective:

What actually happened?

How did we respond to it?

How could we have responded more maturely?

What is the lesson we need to be learning?

The first question is important only to the degree that it helps us review the event objectively. Many people find it hard to remember the actual details of events. They remember selectively, dwelling on certain facts and omitting others. Or they remember creatively, inserting self-serving assumptions and speculations as needed to support their conclusions. Obviously, whenever this kind of distortion occurs, it becomes almost impossible to learn the lesson life is trying to teach us. We must learn objectivity first.

The second and third questions are the more meaningful ones, in that they help us weigh our reaction to this event. This reaction is the heart of our experience, and therefore the primary clue to the lesson we are learning. If we react angrily to the helpful suggestions of others, for example, the lesson is quite clear: we need to examine why we were so threatened by these ideas. If we become depressed on a regular basis without apparent reason, the lesson is a bit more difficult to detect. At some point, we have damaged our response mechanism by being blinded by despair and grimness. As a result, we have dulled our ability to recognize and celebrate our achievements and blessings. By default, we are subject to fits of melancholy and gloom.

Each experience presents a new lesson and must be interpreted in its own light. It is important to understand, however, that the lesson always pertains to us. If we are the type of person who habitually blames everyone else for everything that is wrong, we may not understand this point at first. It is quite likely that the other people involved have lessons to be learned as well. But those are their lessons. They will differ from our lessons. We need not concern ourselves greatly with them. We need to focus instead on the lessons we are learning.

It may well be true that the "other person" is rude and obnoxious. It is easy to believe, in such cases, that we have nothing to learn—after all, there would be no problem at all, if only the other person changed. But this is not true. We would still be unable to deal with rude people! We therefore need to realize that this is an irreplaceable opportunity to learn to cope with all obnoxious people.

Life is economical. It never wastes any experience on us. There is always a lesson to be learned in everything we do. It may be that we do not need to strain or fight so hard for what we are trying to achieve. It could be that we need to build a stonger sense of self-esteem. At other times, life may be calling to us to increase our ability to care for others, nurture their growth, or support them in their endeavors.

If our dominant mood is grimness, life is calling to us to lighten up and learn to express joy. If we never seem to get anything done, life may be calling us to learn to take more initiative. If we keep on dwelling on past hurts, it is reminding us to flush out the garbage of the past and start living in the present.

As we develop the good habit of learning from the lessons of experience, we discover something else. The more we regard life as a textbook, and use it as a primary impetus to our growth, the more we are able to shape the kind of experiences that come to us. In truth, we write the ticket of our destiny far more than most of us realize. We give new structure—and meaning—to the seemingly random experiences of life.

The best way to improve our skills in learning from life is to rehearse our lessons. The natural starting point would be to review a pleasant episode of life. Did we learn anything—or just enjoy ourself? What went right—and why did it? Could we repeat this in the future? What are the hidden meanings of this experience? What positive attitudes sustained us? How much of our spiritual will did we embody? Has this helped us become more attuned to the spiritual self? Have we integrated this lesson into our sense of identity and world view?

Once we become comfortable with this type of rehearsing, we can use it also to review a negative experience. Did we learn anything from this event—or just suffer? Was the event itself the source of our suffering—or our immature reaction to it? How did life challenge us? What did we do to precipitate this crisis? Was there anything we did that made it worse? What should we have learned—physically, emotionally, mentally, and spiritually—from this situation?

Based on these examinations of our experiences, we can then proceed to a more general review: how do we need to change ourself and our world view? How can we improve our self-image? What have we learned about cooperating with other people? What have we learned about cooperating with the higher self?

By probing into the inner depths of the events of life in these ways, we can accelerate our personal growth immensely. The intelligence of life is constantly communing with us, trying to guide us wisely. Our personal experiences are one of the many ways these messages are beamed at us. They are a daily source of support to everyone interested in learning.

5.

Getting the Messages of Life

Everything in life has a tale to tell—a subtle or hidden message that can teach us something new about life, if we have the eyes to see and the ears to hear. Some of these lessons are so subtle that we may very well miss them—at least at first. But the earlier we recognize the lessons our own higher intelligence is trying to point out to us, and learn them, the more rapidly we will progress.

The lessons we need to learn in life are often introduced to us by our higher intelligence in very quiet, nonthreatening ways—as *object lessons* we observe in others, encounter in literature, or discern in nature. A friend, for example, may tell us about a humiliating experience he or she endured as a child—laughing about it from the perspective of adult maturity—just a few days before we find ourself being tested in a similar fashion. Such advance warning is not just a striking coincidence—it is the effort of the higher self to prepare the personality to see the humor, not the pain, in our imminent encounter with humiliation.

Do we get the message? Alas—all too often we do not, because we have not trained ourself to look for these object lessons, study them, and draw from them the insights we need in order to grow. As a result, we frequently must deal with the challenges of life with a severe handicap—the confusion that results from not taking advantage of every opportunity to learn that which we need to know.

Object lessons come in many shapes and sizes. The reason why they are sometimes hard to detect, at least at first, is because they are so common place. The higher self chooses the ordinary interests and resources of our daily life as the stage setting for these lessons. As a result, the average person is tempted to ignore any extra meaning they might have. Even the agent of light must make a concerted effort to discern the meaning and significance of these lessons.

Naturally, the most common resource for object lessons would be the experiences of other people in our lives, not just close friends but also casual acquaintances—even people in the news we do not know. If a co-worker is branded a trouble maker because he undercuts the efforts of others, it might be helpful for us to re-examine our own attitudes toward competitiveness and getting along with colleagues, making adjustments in our attitudes and behavior before we, too, earn a bad reputation. If the stridency of a politician in the news offends us, it might be helpful to evaluate the tone and timber of our own comments about issues we believe in passionately—and how others respond to them.

Groups also provide lots of material for potential object lessons. The difficulties that have arisen in our public schools—drugs, shootings, and so on—should be a solemn object lesson to anyone inclined to believe that discipline obstructs education, rather than enabling it. Even national and international events can serve as this kind of lesson. The exposé of a scandalous mismanagement of government funds, for instance, may also be a warning to make sure that our own handling of entrusted funds is fully without reproach.

Some of the most powerful object lessons are those we encounter in great fiction. An excellent example would be the character of Sybil in Charles William's *The Greater Trumps*, who demonstrates Christ-like qualities of nurturing love in the face of dire threat and powerfully acts out the meaning of redemption. It is hard to read this great novel without being inspired, at least to a degree, to a new recognition of the value of love in the way we treat ourself—and everyone else.

In much the same way, myths are also a good source for object lessons. The story of the twelve labors of Hercules, for instance, is a marvelous portrayal of the fundamental lessons of spiritual mastery each of us must pass as we tread the path. Careful reading will also lead us to some of the deeper meanings behind these lessons—aspects not always apparent to the personality.

Nature is likewise a rich resource of lessons to be learned. Something as simple as a moment's reflection on the way plants convert mud and water into edible vegetables and fruits can inspire us with new insights into the capacity of

65

spirit to transform the mundane into something useful.

Many powerful object lessons can be drawn from the lives of saints, martyrs, and avatars, too. When Paul writes about "a thorn in his side," we are meant to look at our own life and see how the extra burdens we carry through life enable us to pursue our spiritual destiny—for instance, by compelling us to cultivate greater humility, self-discipline, or courage.

Even omens can act as guides to object lessons we need to learn. An omen can be something as simple as seeing our first budding flower in the spring. It is like the herald for the real message—that new opportunities are opening up for us in unexpected places.

Regardless of the source, there is great value in learning from these object lessons. The insights we gain accrue without any pain or involvement by us. We are learning from the good—and bad—examples of others. In a way, these object lessons could be viewed as examples of God's mercy and grace—even when we fail to see them or act on them.

It is therefore important to get into the habit of looking for these object lessons—and teaching ourself how to learn from them. They represent the easiest way for higher intelligence to get its message through to us—if we pay attention! We are often so caught up in the struggles and trauma of life that it is hard to see past our own hurt and injury. In such cases, it may be far easier to learn the value of patience or hope in the context of someone else's struggles, rather than our own.

There is also the obvious limit to what we can personally experience. By expanding our scope of learning to embrace the object lessons occurring around us, we can vastly expand our field of learning.

Because life itself is intelligent, object lessons can be found in almost every experience. The key is learning to interpret the lesson in ways that are helpful and beneficial. There are five basic categories of lessons we can learn:

1. What works—and doesn't work. We may be so caught up in our own anger that we are unable to see how our refusal to forgive someone else is degrading the quality of our own life. But if we can see the same damage occurring in the life of someone else, we may eventually get the message: we will be imprisoned in our own hurt and bitterness until we learn to forgive.

Just so, we may have no idea how silly we appear to others when we become defensive in the face of criticism at work. But when we can see how foolish a co-worker looks, even when defensiveness seems to be justified, we may at last be responsive to the message: there is no dignity in defensiveness.

2. Good examples. We cannot learn to play the piano by listening to a great pianist perform. But if we already know how to play, then watching—and listening—to a great pianist can help us pick up skills and interpretations that will enhance our own ability.

In this regard, parents of unruly children might be well advised to study the object lessons presented by parents of well-mannered, healthy kids.

3. Encouragement. There are times when what we need

is renewed hope and motivation, rather than greater knowledge or insight. At such a time, a television report on someone who regains his health after a nasty bout of cancer may be just the object lesson we need in order to accomplish our goals.

By the same token, the courage of a dying friend may deliver a far more powerful message about facing life than a hundred homilies.

4. Warning. The collapse of a government or the downfall of a particular politician may be just tonight's news. But if it strikes a chord within us, it may also be an object lesson—a warning from higher intelligence that we have pressed our luck too far with others, and our little empire is about to collapse.

5. Shallowness. Many people let the fads and trends of mass consciousness overwhelm their sense of personality. Too much of this kind of susceptibility weakens the ability of the personality to respond to higher intelligence. But it is often hard to see the level to which this susceptibility has grown. In these cases, the only way to get the message through is to bombard us with examples of how superficial the lives of others around them have become—to the point where they see their own shallowness as well.

The basic message of an object lesson is written by our own higher intelligence, the light within us. Examples of this message are then selected and played out for us. These events arise so spontaneously and seem so much a natural part of life, however, that we usually do not suspect that they are lessons. We ignore them.

With object lessons, therefore, the first question always is: "Did we get the message?"

Once this question can be answered in the affirmative, another one arises: "At what level?"

Like any communication from spirit to personality, there can be three levels of meaning in the object lessons the soul presents to us—the literal, the symbolic, and the cosmic.

The **literal** level defines the lesson to be learned. If an unsupervised child runs smack into a pyramid of canned peas in a grocery store, it is a direct message to every kid watching that such uncontrolled behavior will lead to catastrophe every time. Such literal messages spell out the desired behavior in no uncertain terms.

Just so, a moment of carelessness by another driver on the highway may be an object lesson literally warning us to take our own driving responsibilities more seriously.

The **symbolic** level illustrates the inner principle or law of behavior we need to learn. If we are a parent of a rude child, we need to consider how discipline must be built on a structure of intelligence and compassion. Until our child sees the value of discipline within our own character, our commandments will fall on deaf ears. In other words, we need to appreciate the value of a mature character.

The principles of daily living are not just dusty precepts to be acknowledged and paid lip service. They are the key to learning any lesson. These principles will be the same for all people, but will be expressed in many different ways by different individuals. Until these differences are discerned, we may be more confused than helped by object lessons.

Watching a highly-paid ball player work out his frustrations after striking out by trying to destroy the dugout wall with his bat may be an object lesson—but only if we discern the symbolic meaning correctly. The ball player is letting off steam by being overtly destructive—hardly the ideal. We need to see the symbolic beyond the ideal—the *potential* for this player to act with dignity and poise in the face of adversity, even when it is conspicuously absent. It is to these qualities of dignity and poise that we should aspire—and leave the ball player with his frustration and broken bats.

Sometimes we need to penetrate beyond even the symbolic, until we arrive at a transcendent or **cosmic** level of understanding. There is much we can learn about divine love and justice, for instance, in the interaction of people and groups, but the cosmic level of love and justice embraces all of humanity, not just a few chosen people. A good object lesson about divine love, or its absence, can often be drawn from national and international news—or historical, mythological, or religious accounts.

In defining the lesson, however, we must take care to avoid trivializing cosmic love as sentimentality and trivializing cosmic justice as just wanting favors for our side. In this regard, the compassion with which Abraham Lincoln approached the Reconstruction of the country following the Civil War is an object lesson that can inspire the insightful student at all three levels—the literal, the symbolic, and the cosmic.

By their very nature, object lessons are easily missed.

The most important requirement for capitalizing on these lessons, therefore, is simple and direct: *pay attention!*

We must start watching the words and deeds of the people around us—friends, loved ones, colleagues, and acquaintances. This includes reading the news—not just superficial accounts of the news, but the facts and details that provide a larger context for the news. We must nurture our associative mechanism with good fiction and mythology—stories that explore solutions to modern problems, not just ones that give accounts of suffering and protest injustice. In every facet of life, we need to start looking for deeper patterns of meaning.

As we reflect on any given object lesson, we should ask: What does this episode teach us about life?

What divine qualities or virtues does this situation exhibit—perhaps by their conspicuous absence? How can we cultivate them?

What skills or values are lacking? How does this compound the problem? How can we cultivate the missing forces of self-expression?

What larger patterns of life are at work in this example?

What principle, law, or theme of living is being explored? How can we learn to work with this insight on our own?

How can we apply this new knowledge?

These are not always easy questions to answer—and there is no teacher's manual giving a list of right answers in the back. But the effort to understand the hidden messages in the object lessons that come to us will lead us, step by step, to a whole new understanding of life.

As we practice this new method of learning, we must be

sure to work with both good and bad object lessons—lessons that show us how to behave and those that show us the dire consequences of misbehaving. We do not have to invent these lessons, just be patient and let them arise naturally in the course of daily living. The correct posture is attentiveness, plus a willingness to let divine wisdom help us learn.

There are many different kinds of object lessons we can examine. Some of the possibilities include:

- The actions of a friend or colleague.
- A character in a novel or movie.
- An event in national or world news.
- The behavior of a group.
- An example from nature or the animal kingdom.
- A mythic or religious figure.

As we work through the meaning of each lesson for us, its relevance will become obvious. We will not only learn more about our needs for specific types of inner and spiritual growth, but also the remarkable ability of divine intelligence to supply the exact lessons we need.

The best way to honor this new realization, of course, is to act upon these new insights and implement the changes they point us toward.

6.

Learning From Trial and Error

Of all the ways by which human beings learn, the most basic is trial and error. As we stumble through some experience as best we can, ideally we examine how we are doing and what kind of results we are producing. Are we achieving our goals? At what price? Is the price too high? Are we making mistakes? Are we alienating others? How could we have acted more wisely, efficiently, and lovingly?

Humans are not designed to live by theories alone. It is certainly desirable to think about and rehearse our actions in advance, planning the best course we can take. But when it comes to the actual act of *learning*, the abstract must become concrete. Theory must be applied. We must test the assumptions we have made about daily life—and learn to recognize the messages and lessons from our higher intelligence contained within our experiences.

73

Unfortunately, not all people are comfortable learning the lessons of life through trial and error. They assume that they should already know all of life's answers. To their minds, childhood is a time for learning; adulthood is a time for applying what has been learned. They fail to see that learning is a lifelong necessity. All too often, they not only evade the lessons of adulthood but even deny their duty to grow.

There are four basic types of people who are distinctly uncomfortable with the process of learning by trial and error:

• The perfectionist, who cannot tolerate either failure or defect in anyone, including himself or herself—or society. These people are so offended by error that they are a) trapped in arrogance, b) blinded to the simple steps needed to correct the error, and c) unable to accept the lessons being taught.

• The theoretician, who believes that all theories can be applied without adaptation or modification. As a result, he tries to make all of the phenomena of life conform to his favorite theories, rather than reshape the theories to reflect why the world works the way it does. He blinds himself to reality.

• The true believer, who will cling to dogma and catechism long after it proves itself inadequate.

• The guilt-obsessed, who are so consumed with the fact that they have sinned or erred that they do not believe it is possible to adequately atone for their acts, let alone learn from them. They try to replace learning with constant contrition.

The lessons of life do not cease when we become twenty-one. They continue as before. But instead of being lessons rehearsed under the watchful eye of our parents, they are lessons we must acquire on our own, as we experiment with ideas, human relationships, new skills, and our own spiritual quest.

The process of learning through trial and error is always a direct and important part of this ongoing growth. It teaches us just how realistic our ideas, expectations, and beliefs actually are. It keeps us in tune with reality.

Too many people give up learning too quickly. Instead of seeing the challenges of adult life as learning opportunities, they view them more darkly as threats, humiliations, pitfalls, and traps. This creates a basic misunderstanding about life and our responsibility toward it.

This basic misunderstanding is most clearly seen in the way many people define success and failure. They see them as opposite ends of a straight line, their journey beginning at the middle of this hypothetical straight line, and taking them either to the pole of success or the pole of failure. To heaven or hell. To right or wrong.

Nothing could be further from the truth. Success and failure are not polar opposites, constantly waging battle for our soul—or at least our happiness. Success and failure are the two motivating forces within the learning process. Success is the carrot in front of the horse, encouraging it to move forward. Failure is the prod that must be applied when the horse slows down and will go no further. But both work together to help us achieve our goals.

Unfortunately, our society suffers from a near-universal fear of failure. Failure is talked about as something to be avoided at all costs; success, on the other hand, is something to be achieved no matter what the price. These misleading concepts have polarized our understanding of growth—and traumatized many good and decent people.

No true success can ever be built except on a foundation of apparent failures—the certain knowledge of what does not work. Each failure teaches us a lesson that becomes a part of our talent to achieve. If we are alert to these lessons, and actively seek to master them, we can greatly accelerate the speed by which we become successful.

In this context, it may be helpful to realize that many apparent successes are actually more parts failure than triumph. A person who achieves financial success by cheating others is actually creating a foundation of failure, not success. The short term glory he or she enjoys will soon collapse—and no one will be willing to help. Just so, a politician winning a landslide election may feel triumphant, but his success may be more illusion than real if he ends up caught in a web of dishonesty and forced to resign.

We need to borrow from the Chinese the concept that all successes contain the seeds of eventual failure—and all failures contain the seeds of eventual success. No specific event is inherently a success or a failure; success or failure are terms that describe how effectively we harness events for our own growth, development, and service to others.

In other words, success is not just an event—it is also a process. It is a process of increasing our skills and understanding in whatever we are doing, so we can do it better.

It is a process of learning.

It is for this reason that the wise person learns how to learn by trial and error. These trials are not blind stabs in the dark. On the contrary, they should represent the best, most mature level of effort of which we are presently capable. But they are not life or death gambles. They are experiments. If the experiment fails, we can still learn a great deal, by *recovering* from the failure—by learning what works and what does not.

Learning the roles success and failure play in the learning process likewise helps us increase our discernment. If the challenges of life are nothing more sinister than experiments from which we are meant to learn, why then should we be embarrassed if we fail? We should only be embarrassed if we fail to try. Just so, why should we feel guilty about our mistakes? Once we have learned from and corrected them, we should bless them and get on with living.

People who are uncomfortable with the process of learning by trial and error usually end up trying to avoid the battles, confrontations, and crises which generate moments of learning opportunity. They do not want to be humiliated, scorned, or criticized. But those who try to avoid the challenges of life end up with the logical consequence of avoidance: nothing.

When enlightenment is the prize, who in their right mind would be content with nothing?

The other great virtue of the process of learning by trial and error is that it is life's gentle way of commenting on our plans and efforts. It gives us feedback.

As we work toward any goal, we form opinions of how

we are doing. These opinions are often quite useful and accurate, but at times they can also become highly colored by our own personal enthusiasm, confidence, or arrogance. When these personal feelings start to mislead us, we need a blast of feedback to alert us to this problem and force us to rethink our plans, assumptions, priorities, and procedures.

This is not to suggest that all resistance to our initiatives is a divinely-inspired message. We must always evaluate hardships and mishaps in the light of our established goals, standards, and methods. If we remain convinced that all of these things are still worthy, then we should proceed.

But there are other times when criticism from others and the lack of cooperation from life itself sound an alarm for us, trying to get us to see the error of our ways and take steps to correct them. This is the feedback that everyone needs to heed in order to be productive in this world. It should force us to rethink our efforts and make minor revisions and adjustments—or even major overhauls.

This feedback may not be limited just to the effectiveness of our methodology. It may point out the fact that the major problem we must correct is our hostility and pessimism, or the impulsiveness with which we work, or the stubbornness and inflexibility with which we pursue our goals. We might even have the wrong goals!

It may even go deeper still, exposing the fact that while we have the skills that should enable us to achieve success, we lack the insight and level of commitment necessary to reach this goal. If we are trying to touch the depths of the human soul through our art or science, after all, and yet have no genuine contact with these depths ourself—only an intellectual level of understanding and competence—we will constantly meet with setbacks until we correct the underlying problem.

Men and women were not created to be right. We were created to experiment with all of the many variables of life, and through this experimentation, reveal our full potential. This begins with discovering our own range of human self-expression—as a loving, joyful, wise, and generous person. But it extends to discovering the full potential of everything here on earth as well. In this way, we learn to find the light within us and the light within life—and discover what it means to know and express it.

To a large degree, we must find our own way. We can be helped by observing examples of others—as well as by our own intuition. But we are also meant to increase our skill and intelligence by experimenting—by taking intelligent risks that invest our humanity in worthwhile projects and goals.

To put it simply, we are meant to try to act and live the best we know how. This always involves a certain risk. What if "our best" is actually less than the best? But how much of a risk is this in reality? The only parts that are truly at risk are our incompetence and ignorance!

The process of experimenting by trial and error becomes more effective as we cultivate a long-range view of what we are doing and what we are meant to achieve, coupled with a sense of how long it will take. If we start to view our true experiments in life as covering multiple lifetimes and thousands of years, we may gain a much healthier understanding that the risks of this moment in time are well worth taking.

Actually, the process of experimentation is a "no fault" practice. If our experiment works, great. We can go on to the next challenge. But if it fails, or only partially succeeds, that is all right, too—by learning from our difficulties, we will be better prepared to try again—and succeed.

In this light, therefore, it should be clear that the major enemies to our success all lie within us. It is not usually an event of life that defeats us, when we fail; it is our own arrogance, stubborness, laziness, or naïveté. Our conviction that we know exactly what we ought to be doing will inevitably clash with the guidance of the higher self, preventing success.

Nor is it the ferocity of our opposition or competition that usually undermines our efforts; it is more often our own rigidity. Our determination to be always in control of our life makes it next to impossible for the higher self to exercise its rightful measure of influence, which is the key to triumph.

Just so, it is generally not the fickleness of fate that clouds our prospects; it is our own insecurity. It is not the unresponsiveness of mass consciousness to our brilliant ideas; it is our own unrealistic expectations. It is not the corrupt nature of mankind that we must rail against. Instead, we must strengthen our own commitment to be helpful toward all.

It is an integral part of the growth process of every human being to succeed. But to achieve success, we must be willing to experiment and take risks with life. We must be willing to fail—and then be courageous enough to learn the lessons of success that can be built on that foundation of failure.

The process of learning by trial and error is easily mastered by anyone willing to take risks. Fortunately, each of us has plenty of examples, in the form of memories, from which we can learn the basic technique.

Here is a simple exercise:

We begin by picking a failure from our past, then answer these questions in a reflective state of mind:

Why did we fail?

What was our original intent or goal?

Did we define the goal properly?

Did we define failure properly?

What did we do, if anything, to contribute to the failure?

Did this failure stop us from continuing to strive toward our goal?

Did we retreat into self-imposed traps of arrogance, rigidity, insecurity, laziness, or conformity?

Have we since reached our goal?

What have we learned in spite of our presumption of failure? These lessons might include new insights, a deeper sense of maturity, strengthened dedication, a better sense of direction, or even specific qualities of consciousness and skills.

Did this "failure" sow seeds of eventual success?

Should we still be viewing this as a "failure"—or as a valuable lesson in living?

As we review each episode, we should try to cultivate a

deeper appreciation of the benevolent intelligence at work within us, plus a greater measure of compassion for the value of learning by trial and error.

7.

Educating
The Mind

The human mind is like the manager of a modern small business. A manager oversees planning, operations, personnel, and many other aspects of the company. He has great authority to implement goals, plans, and policies. He disciplines and supervises his staff so that the work is completed. He responds to the needs of the customers. In addition, he must abide by the law of the land and adhere to the wishes of the owner. But before the manager does any of these things, *he manages ideas and makes decisions.* Throughout this whole process, he strives always to sustain and increase the efficiency and productivity of the company.

The mind is meant to act in much the same way for the personality. It is designed to be the chief operating officer of our daily self-expression—the guardian of our genius, goodwill, and labor. And like the business manager, before the mind manages anything else, it must manage ideas and decisions.

It is obvious that the mind must learn to interact with the world around it in a knowledgeable, intelligent way. However, it must also become responsive to the direction of the soul as well as the external demands of life, because, like the business manager, the mind is limited by law—divine law and purpose. This is not so much a restriction on the mind as it is the very heart of its authority. The mind is meant to *discover* the guidance of the soul, becoming aware of its purpose and design. The mind needs to *interpret* these abstract insights and translate them into intelligent plans for development through our creative thinking, responsible use of our strengths and abilities, and helpful attitudes. To achieve all this, the mind must also *teach* and *supervise* the emotions and body to cooperate with and obey these decisions—a difficult task, indeed, as the emotions and the body have a tendency to listen to their own urges, while rejecting the control of the mind. And throughout this process, the mind must always strive to sustain and increase the efficiency and productivity of the personality.

There are many businesses that miss the opportunity to grow. They develop bureaucratic infrastructures that suffocate inspiration. They create layers of command which dilute authority and distract employees from their purpose. They fail to remain up-to-date in their use of technology or their approach to market conditions. They become isolated from the rest of the world, unable to respond to the emerging needs of their customers or clients.

In much the same way, many humans miss daily chances to grow mentally. The mind does not automatically fulfill any of the duties just outlined. It must be educated with suitable instruction and trained through proper experience.

In some cases, people miss this chance because they view the mind too materialistically. They confuse the mind for the brain, which it is not. The brain is a physical organ which receives thought impulses from the mind, coordinates them, and then redirects these impulses throughout the physiological system, as needed. It can transmit impulses, but it cannot think. Only the mind can think. It is the mind that must be educated, not the brain. The effort to train the brain is actually a diversion which induces people to overlook educating the mind.

Other people believe that they have, in fact, received the mental training they need in school. Now that they are adults, they know what they need to know, and have no further need for education. Surely this attitude is the origin of the cliché that ignorance is bliss. First of all, very little of modern education actually addresses the development of the mind. Second, and more importantly, any program of education that stifles mental curiosity—by convincing its students that they have learned all they need to know—has failed woefully.

Educating the mind is a lifelong proposition. Public education is meant to give children the tools and the zeal for learning they will need in order to continue growing as adults. If we do not receive this capacity through our formal education, then it is up to each of us individually to supply it.

The mind's ability to learn and expand can never be exhausted. Nor can our need for greater illumination and wisdom—not to mention the mental skills by which we can apply them. Ideally, education teaches us to nurture the impulse to grow in awareness and competence—to explore the unknown, to conquer it, and to make it our own.

Unfortunately, we still fall short of this ideal. Far too many people, like businesses, change only when forced into it. As a result, when they do make an earnest effort to grow, they are unfamiliar with the learning process—and waste much time and make a lot of mistakes through trial and error.

This is the hard way. A far better alternative is to make the training and education of the mind a central part of our daily activities. We need to harness our impulse to grow and learn to direct it—with as much intelligence and wisdom as we can muster.

How should the mind be growing? What constitutes a solid education? The answer lies in understanding the functions the mind is meant to perform.

What is the mind supposed to do? Most people would respond: to think. Technically, this is true. But "thinking" is a far more inclusive process than most of us appreciate. The role of the mind is to be our agent for the exploration and management of the many dimensions within ourself, as well as the many aspects of the world around us. Most people explore only the external world—and only in its material aspects. A few more also explore the physical and emotional dimensions of their personality. Still fewer successfully explore the spiritual dimensions of their individuality and the world. Yet effective thinking and genuine growth must combine all of these levels of exploration.

At its highest level, the mind is meant to explore the light of the soul—the light of divine life—and direct this light into the personality as greater wisdom, maturity, and effectiveness. This is true thinking. It could also be called the act of "enlightenment."

In fact, the mind is not doing its job effectively unless its explorations contact an element of divine light. The mind that "observes" poverty in the world through its own despair, magnifies it with its own sense of inadequacy, and then concludes that there is no hope for the future is not thinking properly. The process of enlightenment is breaking down. It has become the process of self-delusion.

Just so, a mind that is affixed throughout most of the day on utterly petty issues is not thinking competently, either—no matter how intelligently or brilliantly the mind may handle these trivial details. Enlightenment derives from light, not pettiness.

The human mind does not invent or create this light. Light exists as a basic aspect of the mind of God. At first, our contact with the light of divine mind will happen unconsciously. Whole thoughts will suddenly emerge into our conscious awareness without any seeming effort on our part. But as we train the mind to respond fully and alertly to such "gifts," we begin to recognize that the mind is far greater than we had imagined. It contains abstract parts that already know how to interact with light. As we harness these thoughts and work with them, our skills in thinking evolve and become stronger.

It is not the role of the mind, therefore, to invent the answers to life's difficult questions. The mind's job is to focus its curiosity to discover the answers that already exist, in divine intelligence, to ponder on them, and then to apply the conclusions we make to daily living.

This is not an easy lesson to learn, however. The temptation to believe that our own perceptions and opinions are the ultimate reality and authority is overwhelming to some people. Many such people openly believe, for example, that there is no divine life, and are quite smug about it. Yet this opinion, no matter how strongly held, does not enrich their thinking or their life. Instead, it closes their mind to the central reality of life. It makes true thinking—enlightenment—next to impossible.

When we understand the mind as a tool or vehicle for the enlightenment of the personality, then its true usefulness can unfold. We can see that the mind is designed to:

• Explore the world around us, gathering data about it. This could be a scientist gathering information about the laws of physics, a psychologist observing human behavior, or one spouse listening to what the other one is saying. We must learn to examine life objectively, as it truly is—and then search for the divine potential and opportunities within these conditions. This is an important step in training the mind, because most of us gather data emotionally, not mentally, in order to fulfill our preconceptions about life, excuse ourself, or find someone to blame.

• Explore our character. As Pope put it, "The proper

study of mankind is Man." We need to examine our values, goals, feelings, thoughts, and habits. When we come across a helpful element, such as faith, we should study how it links us with divine forces, such as healing and endurance. When we come across a destructive element, such as anger, we need to ask: "What are we missing?" In other words, what divine quality or force—such as compassion—would heal our anger and the situation provoking it? Always, our goal in this self-examination should be a greater contact with enlightenment—never an exercise in self-indulgence or the justification of immature behavior.

• Explore the laws of life. The events of life, taken together, become a great textbook in the education of the mind. Even though the series of events which befall us may seem random, there is a thread of meaning which runs through all of them. The mind can learn to look for this thread and interpret it, thereby revealing the influence of the law of cause and effect on our life. People who rely on their emotions to understand life generally draw a negative conclusion from reading these messages—for example, that God is angry with them and punishing them for their sins. The mind can help us rise above such misconceptions and discern a clearer sense of meaning, by examining the events of life in the context of divine law. The mind can show us, for instance, that guilt and fear can do nothing productive, yet will inevitably tear apart the health of the emotions and physical body.

• Integrate past experiences with present need. Once we have used the mind to inventory our memories, habits, and abilities, we can look for parallels between the present and the past, so that we may draw on strengths and skills learned long ago to meet the needs of current life—or, conversely, to make sure that we do not repeat the errors of the past yet another time.

• Integrate purpose with thought and feeling. Many problems of human living, especially in marriages, child-raising, and work, arise because we forget to honor the primary purpose of the activity. We get angry at our spouse and precipitate an argument, even though the substance of disagreement is petty and insignificant in comparison to the larger purpose of our relationship and commitment. The mind is ideally suited to comprehend the purpose of all of our activities, so that we can remain focused in genuine issues at moments of conflict, instead of allowing ourself to be drawn into insignificant distractions.

• Supervise the repair of thoughts and feelings. People who are focused in their emotions do not believe hurt feelings can be repaired; once victimized, they remain that way the rest of their lives. In truth, the enlightened mind has the ability to heal and repair wounded thoughts and feelings alike. These elements of consciousness can only be hurt if we are deficient in the strength of a divine element—such as inner patterns of goodwill, wisdom, joy, or peace. The mind can easily learn to attune to these divine qualities, absorb them, and then direct them to heal the wound or injury. Forgiveness, healing, and redemption are all based on the use of the mind in this way.

• Update beliefs, convictions, values, and priorities. The momentum of life is constantly forcing us to change. Yet many of us fail to keep pace with these changes, trying to approach our lives with values and beliefs shaped much earlier, even as a child. The mind needs to be trained to help us revise and update our views, hopes, goals, traits, and priorities.

• Direct plans into activity. The most enlightened plans are useless unless they are set in motion. Many fine people have yet to learn that unless good intentions are acted on, they produce no results. The emotions and the body tend to ignore plans for change; it is the job of the mind to remain vigilant and insure that plans are implemented. This requires training the mind in the intelligent direction of the spiritual will.

• Listen and respond to feedback. Life is continually giving us feedback to our efforts to grow and contribute. The emotions, for example, tend to respond to challenges defensively. Our fear tells us the risk is too great. Our anger tells us someone else is to blame. The mind needs to learn how to evaluate accurately what happens to us, as well as the false feedback of emotional reactiveness. This requires teaching the mind to be more discerning—to look beyond our usual reactions.

• Overcome resistance to change. Any effort to change major patterns of thought and attitude will incite resistance, either from our subconscious or mass consciousness. The mind needs to learn how to tap the strength and will of the primary purpose of any activity to defeat such resistance.

• Discipline attention. Many people are slaves to any thought, feeling, or sensation that emerges in their awareness. This is the sign of an untrained mind. The mind has the ability to focus and hold attention on any subject or issue. This capacity gives us the ability to stabilize our concentration and, when appropriate, to deepen it, contacting the essence of our inquiry.

• Oversee the emotions. Left to their own initiative, the emotions will react automatically to any impression, real or imagined. The result is often excitement or even chaos. The emotions can reach their peak effectiveness only when supervised by the mind, so that we use the emotions to add warmth and attractiveness to our activities, communications, and relationships. In a crisis, for example, the uncontrolled emotions will panic. Emotions governed by an enlightened mind, on the other hand, will add faith to our determination to regain control and hope to our positive expectations.

• Regulate the power to act. The ability of the personality to act effectively can be dissipated by even the slightest disturbance—irritability, fatigue, or doubt. The mind, however, can be trained to appreciate the value of perseverance and to discipline the personality to finish its work.

• Perform sentry duty. As human beings, we are constantly bombarded by propaganda, misinformation, and even the malice and jealousy of others. It is the mind's duty, when properly trained, to recognize and reject these corrupting ideas and influences.

In performing these various duties, the mind is meant to act as nothing less than the agent of the soul—the agent of light. As a result, the importance of the mind to the higher self, as well as the personality, is far greater than most people imagine. The educated mind has power in its own right, but also serves as the representative of the soul. As such it is a gateway of nearly unlimited love, power, wisdom, joy, and peace.

The educated mind therefore deserves far more respect than many people have previously given it, whether it is the Easterner who views the mind as a slayer, because he can only see its concrete functions, or the emotionally-focused person who rates the spontaneous, unthinking use of the emotions as much higher and nobler than the mind. Both of these views are naïve and smallminded, however, because they exclude any recognition of how the mature mind works.

Teaching the mind to recognize and activate its potential should be the cornerstone of any intelligent program of education.

In most cases, the human mind is not taught how to think; instead, it is programmed with rules, tricks, and gimmicks which, when applied to problems, *simulate* the process of thinking. In an art appreciation class, for instance, the mind may be taught to recognize what a majority of art experts consider to be beauty; it is probably not taught how to discern beauty as an abstract, divine reality—or to transform this beauty into an artistic vision, and then bring it into expression through painting, sculpture, or even personal behavior.

The rules, gimmicks, and tricks are valuable, of course—to the concrete mind. But the heart of educating the mind must involve reaching toward the abstract levels—to the fringes of spirit—and learning to interact with the archetypal ideas we find there. To reach enlightenment, we need to teach the mind to respond to the summons of spirit—and educate it in what to do with this knowledge or awareness when the connection is made.

It is therefore important to look at educating the mind in each of its three major categories of activity—exploration, interpretation, and application.

Exploration. We best teach the mind to explore by pushing it to go beyond current limits, whatever they are:

• Beyond the apparent significance of events, so that we learn to recognize and understand the inner patterns and meanings of those events. We may feel betrayed by a friend, and yet this betrayal may simultaneously force us to look at life in a far more enlightened and generous way. The personal lessons we have learned will end up being far more important than the act of betrayal.

• Beyond the mundane interpretation of life, so that the mind will discover the archetypal realities at work. There is a fundamental difference, for example, between the justice administered in our courts of law and the divine archetype of justice. The mind must learn to look beyond the limitations of human justice in order to understand and be inspired by its higher counterpart.

• Beyond the puzzling events of life, to discover universal order. Being fired at work may induce confusion and depression—but it may also hide an inner destiny which is pushing us toward far more favorable circumstances and greater fulfillment.

• Beyond our personalized sense of selfhood, to discover who we truly are—as an agent of light. Our personal sense of who we are tends to be tied to possessions, friends, and earthbound events and sensations. Our links with divine life and light greatly transcend all of these.

• Beyond the superficial focus of our worries, to discover the larger meaning of life. We tend to obsess about our worries and resentments, even though the vast bulk of them are exaggerated or unrealistic. It would be far better to train the mind to honor our larger purpose for health, growth, and creativity. Even a small improvement in this way would produce a big turnaround.

Modern education notoriously fails to encourage these levels of exploration. As a result, we must devise our own programs and regimens for training the mind to explore. Even then, however, we must recognize that some explorations can be misdirected. Certain feminists, for example, are very much interested in exploring how men are sexists—but have no interest at all in exploring how women are. Just so, we often use our preconceptions and biases to initiate self-fulfilling explorations. There can also be the temptation to confuse entertainment for education—by exploring the psychic planes, for example, in search of the latest fashions among spooks!

The mind deserves something much better. It must learn to conduct all explorations with balance and objectivity—and to search out what is genuine and permanent, not transitory and one-sided.

Interpretation. Correctly used, the emotions reflect the beauty and peace of divine life in our self-expression. But the mind is designed to do far more than reflect. Once it has contacted any divine archetypal force, it is meant to interpret it and restate it as appropriate for our own life and projects.

Indeed, our own character and self-expression are the primary laboratories in which we train the mind in proper interpretation. A crisis at work, for instance, may force us to review what needs to be changed in our expectations, work habits, or interactions with others. We begin by carefully reviewing and assessing the feedback, both overt and subtle, we have received from others, and then resolve the problem based on the guiding vision of the higher self. We strive to discover what spiritual quality would enable us to manage this problem effectively, if we could tap it. Next, we concentrate on this divine quality, until our whole awareness resounds with it. At this point, the work of interpretation leads to integration, as we seek to learn how we can translate this divine quality into an attitude, habit, or skill that we can infuse into our basic character and daily behavior.

This basic approach can be used for integrating any divine quality into our character and self-expression:

• Integrating lessons learned in the past with current needs.

• Integrating new insights with ongoing plans.

• Integrating love and joy into our emotions.

• Integrating a new sense of purpose into our daily thoughts, feelings, and intentions.

• Integrating universal forces such as justice and order into our sense of duty and commitment.

• Integrating the light of the mind with the light of the soul.

Application. The third step in educating the mind is training it to apply these interpretations in practical ways in life. Many people regard thinking as an abstract exercise which requires no application. They forget what Edgar Cayce so succinctly stated, that "the mind is the builder." Ideas are meaningless unless they are directed at worthwhile achievements. We should think always with the expectation of creating something with our knowledge. Otherwise, we short-circuit the thinking process.

Applying ideas requires a great deal of effort. It takes only a few moments to conceive an idea for a project; it can easily take years—perhaps even a lifetime—to consummate it. Some of the primary lessons the mind needs to learn in this regard are:

• Translating goals into a plan of action—and results. In order to apply ideas, we must concentrate the nature and power of a vast abstract idea into specific concrete activities. When Albert Schweitzer conceived the idea of taking medical science to the African jungle, it was no easy matter to apply it. First, he had to go to medical school and learn the skills to be a doctor. Next, he had to raise funds to support his venture. Third, he had to travel to Africa, establish a clinic, and then convince the inhabitants to let him treat their physical ailments.

• Managing our anger, fear, discouragement, and doubts. The single greatest possibility for distortion or resistance in applying ideas lies in our own emotions. We can sabotage inspired plans by letting anger, doubt, or self-pity take our goals and intentions hostage. Unless we know our emotions thoroughly and can control them with the mind, we will be very erratic in any effort at application.

• Resisting procrastination. It is never easy to implement new ideas; it is always easier to sustain the status quo—or do nothing at all. The temptation to give in to fears or be overwhelmed by perfectionism is always a strong and real one, unless the mind has been trained to be pragmatic and stay focused in the work ahead—and the higher purpose we serve.

• Maintaining our dedication to constructive purpose. Great ideas are filled with all the power we need in order to implement them. But we must translate the power along with the thought. It is therefore important to train the mind to constantly renew its sense of purpose and determination to apply our noble ideas.

• Monitoring progress. Often, we make the right choice in some issue, only to implement the decision in a thoughtless, irrational way. The mind must be trained to gather and protect our resources and anticipate obstacles and setbacks. It needs to learn to install reviews and quality checks at every stage of implementing ideas.

Not all of these lessons need to be learned at once, of course. But together, they represent a comprehensive curriculum for training the mind in effective thinking—for training the mind to become a proper agent of light.

We can get started in our personal program to train the mind by employing a simple exercise: remembering something that has irritated us. We might be prone to dismiss the incident as trivial; instead, we should take the time to explore it thoroughly, looking to see if it has a meaningful message for us.

Our investigation begins by exploring the broader patterns in which this incident occurred. What actually irritated us? Was it only the situation—or was it something within our own character that overreacted? What is our actual weakness? What mature, spiritual quality would eliminate this weakness, if we possessed it? What spiritual principles are at work? Are there other occasions when we did not cooperate with these spiritual forces?

Once our exploration has led us to the spiritual quality we need, our efforts turn to interpretation. If our mind and heart were filled with this divine quality, how would it alter our view? What new or revised beliefs would it lead to? How would these changes benefit our life? How can we best honor this quality in our daily life? What price will we pay if we fail to make the change?

Having understood the changes that need to be made, all that remains is the actual work of application. Where do we start—what are the first few steps? How are we apt to distort our intent? What other elements may sabotage our effort? What is the best way to keep motivated? How must we focus our priorities, emotions, and energies? If we make this change, will it be necessary to make others?

The regular use of this exercise will train the mind in all of the basic steps of true thinking.

8.

Educating The Emotions

When most adults become enmeshed in a struggle or crisis, it is generally their emotions which stir up the greatest measure of mischief and suffering for them. Their concern with injustice may begin with a mental perception, but it is fueled into outrage by feelings of anger. Their sense of loss may be based in physical reality, but it is magnified by feelings of grief. Their indecisiveness may be triggered by unclear priorities or a lack of facts, but the worry which paralyzes them is a product of emotional brooding.

There is no question that unpleasant events happen to us. But prolonged resentment, anxiety, and grief are not meant to be part of mature living. On the contrary, we are meant to meet adversity with strength, courage, wisdom, poise, and a love for the ideal. Occasionally, we do. But most of the time we regress into emotional reactiveness, burrowing ourselves in a mass of fury, panic, guilt, self-pity or despondency.

Why do we abuse ourselves in this way? The answer is simple. We have failed to recognize that our emotions need to grow up and become mature, just as the body and mind do. We need to learn that the types of behavior which may be acceptable in children are not desirable as adults. We also need to discover that the emotions are just one facet of the personality, a tool for self-expression—not the heart of our character. As such, they can be supervised by our self-control, guided by our common sense, and enriched by our joy and love.

Actually, most people do not understand the vast difference between the *typical* and the *ideal* use of the emotions. Nor are they aware that the emotions can be purified and refined through the regular practice of specific routines of self-control. In fact, most people hold entirely erroneous views of the emotions and the role they play. When a problem arises, they react emotionally, often behaving no better than five-year-olds. They blindly discount the significance of their own immaturity by over-reacting to trivial events. They use anger to project blame, thereby evading responsibility. As a result, they ignore the role they have played in their latest eruption.

Such abuse of the emotions is far more widespread than an isolated case here and there. As a society, we have embraced a number of serious distortions about the emotions and their use. In many cases, in fact, society has come to accept these distortions as "normal."

101

The first step in correcting this problem is to realize that our emotions are meant to be trained to honor our highest good and become an agent for the soul's expression of light on earth. Mature human emotions—ones that have been carefully purified and disciplined—have the potential to be authentic expressions of the divine qualities of goodwill, joy, peace, harmony, beauty, and grace.

An example of this kind of emotional maturity would be the character of Amrita in Talbot Mundy's extraordinary novel, *Black Light*. Amrita faces the probability that she will be forced to leave the ashram in which she grew up and embark on a dangerous and uncertain future. Nevertheless, she faces this possibility with serenity, hope, and forgiveness, in stark contrast to the average human reaction of hatred, self-pity, and fear.

A mature set of emotions represents more than just the expression of the divine ideal, however. They must be purged of habits that would foul our self-expression. We need to be able to curb reactiveness, impulsiveness, and self-centeredness, whether they arise from within our own immaturity—or out of mass consciousness. We must be able to calm the emotions at will and hold them quiet, so that we can perceive and accept guidance and direction from the soul without distortion.

The spiritual design for emotions is to reflect and express the light and love of the soul. As such, our emotions are meant to play a *subordinate* role in the life of the personality—not supplant or obscure our higher values and principles. Emotions are a necessary part of our self-expression; they let us color and enrich the tone of our actions. Mature emotions are meant to honor the best and noblest within us, not be a slave to defending us against enemies, threats, and losses.

There are "experts" who would claim that the emotions are more important than our mind. These people overrate the role of the emotions because of the obvious importance of acting with goodwill and kindness. They also assume that anger is a necessary defense against the threats of life. But kindness without intelligence can spell disaster. Love without principle can lead to terrifying consequences. And anger corrupts our self-expression.

Simply put, we are not meant to trust or follow our gut feelings in the midst of crisis. We are designed to respond to and embody the light of the soul.

Which means educating the emotions.

The first major step in educating the emotions is to learn about the spiritual forces of life and to teach the emotions to embody them—qualities such as goodwill, compassion, joy, harmony, beauty, nobility, courage, peace, charity, reverence, and optimism.

These qualities cannot just be picked up by our feelings and added to our moods, however. They must be translated into appropriate attitudes and beliefs, then integrated into our daily habits of self-expression. A quality such as goodwill, for example, cannot just be annexed and expressed as "feeling good" about events and life. We must translate divine goodwill into a personal spirit of helpfulness and a respect for the goodness within others. Just so, the joy of the soul must be translated into a steady cheerfulness in

103

our outlook; the harmony of spirit must be recast as cooperation with others as we strive toward common goals.

In working with these spiritual energies, we must see that they are clearly incompatible with negative human feelings—feelings that befoul, not enrich us. These include anger, hatred, jealousy, worry, fear, impatience, guilt, grief, and despair. These feelings do not exist in spiritual realms. As such, they can play no role in any mature set of emotions. They must be healed, not justified—and eventually eradicated—first from our self, and then from the emotions of humanity as a whole.

Some people believe such strictness is a bit severe. But the truth of the matter is clear. Love and hate can cohabit in our character only by creating unwholesome schisms within us. As long as we hold onto vestiges of hate, resentment, or vengeance, we cannot cultivate a genuine, full expression of love and goodwill, let alone experience inner peace. We must learn to understand more fully—and to forgive.

The same is true for the whole spectrum of emotion. Peace cannot exist where there is stress and worry. Love cannot flourish where there is jealousy. Beauty cannot prosper where there is ugliness. In order to respond to divine qualities, we must first educate the emotions to outgrow all negative feelings.

We must also recognize the need to outgrow what might be called "baby emotions"—feelings that are safe and sanitized, but only a pale imitation of true spiritual forces. Examples of baby emotions would be sweetness, niceness, blandness, numbness, gentleness, and wishfulness. There may be nothing overtly wrong with these feelings, but they trap us in a superficial level of living that frequently excludes the life of spirit. If we settle for just being nice, we may never learn what it means to express goodwill. If we retreat into numbness at the first sign of stress, we may never learn the power of peace to conquer it. If we substitute wishfulness for faith, we will never tap the power of spirit.

We must therefore use our educated mind to explore the nature of the divine qualities that are meant to be the keystones for our emotions—goodwill, peace, joy, and harmony. Once we have a reasonable understanding of them, we must then define how to express them emotionally in the context of our life.

So far, our work has been largely theoretical. It is likely to remain at this level unless we can compel the emotions to adopt these new patterns. Therefore, our next step in educating the emotions is more pragmatic. We need to find the inner motivation:

• To transform anger into compassion—recognizing the value, for example, of using skill and confidence instead of intimidation to be strong and persuasive. Anger is just another burden that keeps us in a grumpy mood; forgiveness helps us relieve it.

• To transform doubt into faith. We need to see that common sense and knowledge will protect us from deception better than doubt or anxiety. Our life will work better without the doubt that keeps us uncertain and anxious.

• To transform irritability into patience. We need to see that calmness is not numbness—it is relaxed alertness.

It helps us preserve self-control in stressful times and spares us unnecessary frustration.

Girded with these motivations, we can pursue the necessary transformation of our feelings. Acting on the intent to become more kind, faithful, and tolerant, we can make an investment in our personal emotional enrichment. This transformation occurs day by day, as we make the effort to demonstrate compassion, joy, and harmony by being more:

- Supportive to our loved ones.
- Enthusiastic about our work and duties.
- Optimistic about improving our life.
- Grateful for our blessings and opportunities.

This work of transforming the emotions from a reactive, negative attitude toward life to a positive, affirmative, and joyful attitude is an educational process that never ends. We can never exhaust our potential to enrich and ennoble ourselves.

It is not enough, however, just to make a connection with spiritual forces and let them flow through our transformed emotions. Unless we exercise a constant measure of control, even healthy emotions can run amok. Too much enthusiasm, for instance, can be far more dangerous to our well-being than too little.

Unregulated emotions are inherently fluid and unstable. They tend to become reactive and impulsive. Many people think this reactiveness is perfectly normal and that spontaneous impulses are healthy, but this is not so. On the contrary, it is only the uncontrolled gushing of an unredeemed, wild emotional force that is storming through our personality like a tornado charging across the plains. The reactive person is an individual who can easily become possessed by panic, fear, doubt, malice, or excessive sadness, and not know how to turn it off.

Obviously, these emotional storms need to be controlled and disciplined, lest they eclipse the light of the soul. The emotions need to be educated in spiritual obedience. Of course, this suggestion infuriates many "experts." They fret about harming the emotions by suppressing them—or protest that fear and anger are necessary in order to cope with the very real threats and dangers of life. Yet it should be obvious that knowledge, skill, and courage are far more effective shields against danger than a wild, impulsive feeling such as fear.

It is perfectly reasonable to expect to educate the emotions in basic skills. If the mind were left untrained, after all, it would never learn to read or write. It would have little value. Just so, the emotions have little constructive value—and a lot of destructive potential—until we educate them properly. Unless carefully trained, the emotions tend to revert to their natural primitive state. The process of human civilization is one of teaching people to rise out of their natural state, not revert to it.

Understanding the need for controlling the emotions is not the same as achieving it, however. The emotions have absolutely no capacity to control themselves. When given the chance, they will always strive for excitement, responding to the urges and pulls of their own innate sensations— the desire for comfort, sex, security, attention, and pleasure. The source of control and authority over the emotions must therefore come from somewhere other than our feelings—from our common sense, guided by the conscious knowledge of our highest good and by elements of spirit.

It must be emphasized that controlling the emotions is in no way the same as suppressing them. The emotions remain in force, capable of acting with full vitality. We are merely regulating their quality and expression, stressing the divinely-inspired ones and not the negative, harmful ones.

This measure of control develops by combining the understanding mind with the purposeful will to generate intelligent values, priorities, and goals. Each of these provide direction in how to express ourself emotionally. By understanding the value of acting with dignity, for instance, we can grasp the need to act with poise and patience, rather than arrogance. By understanding the value of co-operation, we learn to act with tolerance and affection, rather than hostility and distrust. The more persistent and consistent we are in pursuing these new directions, the more effectively we will train our emotions to conform to our highest good and, in time, our spiritual self.

Some people, of course, believe that all we need to do is become more loving. But an uncontrolled expression of love can easily lead to permissiveness, where there is little or no penalty for dishonesty, incompetence, or rudeness. Our efforts to love must be dedicated to the highest good— not merely our perpetual comfort and convenience. Love, therefore, must be held in focus by the understanding mind and directed by the skillful will.

The third major way we must train the emotions is to coordinate them with our highest values and common sense. The emotions are not meant to be the ruler of the personality—nor even the star performer. The emotions are designed to be a key part of the personality "team"—along with the body, the mind, and the personal will. The work of education is to train each of these four units 1) to live up to its innate design, 2) to learn to work with one another, and 3) to respond to the purpose of the soul.

Because the emotions are often rebellious, this lesson can be a most difficult one. We may have to suffer through repeated internal crises—a poor self-image, excessive guilt, and many other forms of emotional turmoil—before we realize the simple truth that the emotions must be subordinated to the plans and priorities of the enlightened mind and spirit.

The determination to make this submission begins to develop as we come to comprehend that the soul *always* acts with goodwill, joy, nobility, peace, and harmony; it never stoops to indulge in anger, fear, guilt, or despair. If the higher self keeps to this high and noble road, how could it possibly be in our best interest to let the emotions do otherwise?

In point of fact, the human emotions are designed to be a vehicle for expressing the same qualities in the material world that the soul expresses in the subtle worlds. When properly educated, they are able to carry out this noble mission.

The emotions play a very important part in our self-expression. If we are an artist working on a painting, we need to nurture this masterwork with a refined measure of the enthusiasm, joy, and love of the soul. Only the educated emotions can do this.

If we are a parent or teacher responsible for the growth of children, we need to teach, lead, and support them with the sublime care, nobility, and love of the soul. Only the educated emotions can do so.

If we are a leader, we need to reveal the next step forward in growth and development for those who follow us. To do this, we must be able to touch our followers with the presence, dynamic vision, and strength of the soul. Only the educated emotions can do it.

If we are surrounded by selfishness—our own or that of others—we need the inclusiveness, goodwill, and harmony of the soul to combat and redeem it. Only the educated emotions can provide this.

Our emotions learn to provide these qualities by submitting to the love, wisdom, and will of the soul—as we dedicate ourself to expressing the divine qualities of the soul as completely and as perfectly as possible.

Human emotions are the primary vehicle through which such qualities as cheerfulness, harmony, and contentment can be expressed in our life—and the world. Immature, untutored emotions are quite incapable of expressing these qualities, even in favorable circumstances. But properly trained emotions can greatly enrich the quality of life.

A simple exercise can aid us in the work of educating our emotions to live up to their design. We begin by selecting a feeling we want to change.

It is not necessary to review in depth this emotion or the events associated with it. We should focus instead on the spiritual quality or ability that needs to be cultivated in order to reform this emotion and its expression. For resentment, it would be tolerance and forgiveness. For despair, optimism and faith in ourself. For fear, confidence. For guilt, faith in our worth and determination to do better.

Once we achieve this focus, we need to summon and saturate ourself with this healing spiritual quality—for example, tolerance and goodwill. To do this, we need to become more attuned to our soul through meditation, invocation, or prayer.

Having become immersed in this divine force, we need to reflect on how this force wants to be expressed in our life, through our outlook, attitudes, and intentions. How do we need to revise our values, beliefs, and goals so as to embody this divine force more completely? How can we express this divine force in practical ways to improve our relations with others? To accept what we cannot change? To manage our responsibilities more gracefully?

We must also direct this divine force into our personal memories and associations to flush away the poisons of resentment or guilt, whichever we are working to heal.

9.

Educating
The Will

Few aspects of the spiritualized personality have been so consistently misunderstood as the will. For some reason—perhaps the common usage of the word "willfulness" to mean spiteful—the average person tends to equate "will" with self-centered, deliberate acts of rudeness or domination. As a result, when we refer to someone as "strong in will," we generally do not mean it as a compliment. Instead, we are suggesting that this person is pushy, an arrogant know-it-all, insensitive to others, egotistical and self-absorbed, a control freak, impatient and irritable, imperious, or rigid and stubborn.

This is unfortunate, because the true nature of the will bears no resemblance to these common distortions. The will is spirit's vehicle for infusing our activities with the power and direction to reach our goals; for imposing order on the personality and its self-expression; for investing new utility into our ability to heal, act, and work; for persevering in the face of opposition; and for putting a stop to the angry or selfish reactions of the personality.

Obviously, these dimensions of the will are not commonly taught, either by religion, education, or family. Incredible as it may seem—especially since the Christ clearly stated the importance of the will in the last days of His ministry—the will is not even regarded as a major facet of human awareness or self-expression. We talk glibly about the need to cultivate love and wisdom and their many derivatives, but remain largely ignorant of the spiritual will and its uses.

In fact, the little we have been taught about the will has been either misleading or useless. The few scholars who have tried to define it have ended up exploring the wrong end of human psychology, approaching the will as though it were a combination of the personal intellect and desires. They have left out the spiritual reality of the will entirely. Likewise, the many theologians who have felt obliged to opine on the subject have bypassed the spiritualized will, preferring to focus on pride and the need for humility instead. They have all but crippled our study of the will—then instructed us to deny our personal will and supplant it with God's, surrendering all sense of initiative, purpose, and direction. As a result, we are supposed to be passive to the will of God, whatever it may be, on the grounds that this will fulfill our obligation and birthright—which it does not!

The will is one of the three great aspects of all life. As

such, it is part of the trinity of the Godhead, correspond-
ing to the life of the Father, just as love corresponds to the
Christ and active intelligence corresponds to the Mother
or Holy Spirit. The will is nothing less than the force of
purpose in divine creation—the great power that made all
things and continues to sustain them, driving them to fulfill the Plan of God. But this does not limit the will to the
scope and life of God. The triune nature of God mani-
fested in order to pursue the work of Creation. Each part
of this trinity is therefore invested in the "outer" levels
of divine activity—first, in the level of our soul or spiritual essence, and second, in the levels of the personality,
the world of forms. For this reason, we can expect to find
the evidence that the will is active and exerting its influence at both the inner and the outer levels of our being,
even if we have not yet developed the perception to grasp
it fully.

It is surely odd that anything this central to life should
be almost universally overlooked in the education of mankind, but it has been. The reason why is obvious: even the
best thinkers have been unable to put their mental arms
around this force and embrace it. After the great sermons
of the Christ, the first truly intelligent comment on the
subject of the will was not made until Descartes, who recognized the will as something greater than the mind, rather
than a combination of mind and desire. Since then, the
issue of the will has been largely tossed aside. When dis-
cussed at all, it has been primarily in arguments about "free
will," which in effect distorts our whole understanding of
the subject.

This dreadful situation will not change much until we recognize the need to incorporate meaningful lessons on the will into the framework of our education—at the very least, into the education of the agent of light, if not also into the education of the average human being, through school, church, and family.

The expansion of education in this way would enrich our lives in many ways, most of which are not currently being addressed educationally. It would:

• Give us a means for linking our thoughts and even our feelings to purpose and design.

• Provide us with a source of authority and self-control which could be harnessed to redirect our own impulses and immature habits.

• Expose us to an inner source of power that can help us remain steadfast in the face of obstacles and crises and lead a productive life—not just survive.

• Provide us with a means for resisting the influences of the dark areas of mass consciousness and the forces of materialism.

• Cultivate within our character a dedication to the highest, most noble purpose of life. Like faith, this dedication becomes a strong link to divine life.

• Teach us to become self-starting, capable of initiating new lines of activity.

• Awaken us to a deeper respect for the true power of our spiritual design for wholeness.

• Help guide us in developing a set of limits and standards for ourself and our activities.

• Lead us to a more refined sense of responsibility.

For many of these lessons, we will have to seek out and find instruction on our own. We will have to be taught these lessons by the master within us—the soul. Then, as we learn, we can share these lessons with fellow agents of light and family members. As they in turn teach others, gradually lessons about this tremendous force will seep into humanity.

Eventually, when sufficient numbers of mankind demand this instruction, the formal branches of education will respond. This is always the way the spiritual will works—first the few, then the many.

We tend to think that God used the will only to initiate the work of Creation—that during the long unfoldment of evolution, the will stays largely in the background. This picture is not strictly true. God uses the will constantly to sustain the entire process of evolution, to hold steadfastly to the purpose He has set before Himself.

Divine will can be known directly—intuitively—at abstract levels of spirit. It usually cannot be *transferred* directly into our self-expression, but it can be *translated,* as a seed of powerful and noble purpose that will grow in our character, if we nurture it.

In large part, this is because God's will for us is focused in vast schemes for the destined perfection of the whole race of humanity, not in each of us as an individual. Our educational focus as an agent of light must therefore be in the process of transcending personal needs and growth and entering into the larger realm of fulfilling the purpose of mankind. There is great power in the spiritual will, but it cannot be tapped as long as we are guided largely by selfish, desire-based concerns.

In this regard, we must understand that the will is not activated by mere wishing. We interact with the will by dedicating ourself to meaningful plans and goals. The major lessons of educating the will, therefore, can be divided into three steps.

1. Learning to discern the noble purpose of human life, our life, or any specific trend of life. If we believe that human life is just a fluke of random selection, we have no basis for harnessing the will. The same holds true if we believe that our own life has no purpose except to make us suffer. But if we have learned that there is a spiritual purpose behind the struggles of humanity in general and ourself in specific, then we can create an infrastructure of values and intelligence that slowly reveals to us the source of all power, direction, and action. This source is the will. At its most basic level, it is the will to life. This becomes differentiated into the will to love, the will to create, and the will to serve. As we tap into it, by focusing on the purpose of the trends of our life, the direction of will becomes even more finite: the will to know, the will to act, the will to achieve.

The personality, of course, may choose to serve its own purposes—i.e., its selfish ambitions and wants. Such willfulness, however, only serves to limit and restrict us—and get us into mischief. Our personal will has no real power beyond our earthbound desires. *Until we learn, as a personality, to want what God wants for us, we will have no effective link with divine sources!*

117

In order to channel the power of the spiritual will safely, the personality must therefore be well prepared, lest the pursuit of the will become destructive. The most important requirement of the personality is that it be able to work impersonally, ethically, and responsibly. Its goal in seeking out the will should be to energize and contribute to the fulfillment of noble purpose in living.

In fact, there is no point in pursuing the will until we have established a clear sense of responsibility:

• The responsibility to grow—to pursue maturity more than comfort.

• The responsibility to fulfill our domestic and career duties to their highest degrees—not just survive.

• The responsibility to discern and harness opportunities that come to us—to show initiative and creativity more than concern for risks and the status quo.

Until we can fulfill these responsibilities without question or regret, we will run a very real danger of short-circuiting the will.

At this stage of education and religious development, therefore, the primary lessons of the will involve teaching people that a) the spiritual will exists, b) our skillful cooperation and effort are needed to fulfill it, and c) that developing a strong sense of personal responsibility is the best way to prepare ourselves to be touched by the power of the will.

2. Building an unshakeable conviction that the universe is essentially benevolent. At their deepest roots, there is something fundamentally good about human nature, civilization, and God. No matter how much misery and misfortune we encounter in life, we must develop the eyes to see beyond the outer appearance and recognize the hand of divine benevolence at inner levels, painting a masterwork of growth, joy, and beauty, both in human character and culture.

Many academics and theologians are openly dubious about the benevolence of life. Even people who consider themselves to be agents of life may also be skeptical. In fact, the moment they trip and stumble as they tread the path, pessimistic doubts about God's intentions and fundamental goodness begin to emerge in their imaginations. Such doubts must be confronted and eliminated, as must all traces of pessimism; in their place, we must cultivate an unshakeable belief in the divine undercurrent of goodwill and compassion that infuses all of life. Without this change, any attempt to develop the will could lead to self-sabotage, by empowering our tendency to brood, blame, and criticize.

The need to know, beyond all doubt, that life is benevolent is not an optional lesson. It is a prerequisite.

3. Developing an active link with the spiritual will. In addition to being focused in benevolence, we must be dedicated to honoring the divine pattern and plan in every facet of life. This dedication establishes a link between our daily activities and the noble purpose or intent of those activities. As this link grows, we will gradually discover the capacity to interact with the spiritual will.

We therefore need to ponder the question: what does life ultimately expect us to achieve? This may seem to be almost unanswerable, but it is not as difficult as it appears at first. Whatever our primary duties may be, we need to discern the archetypal purpose they serve, not just as we perceive it, but as it affects all of humanity.

In order to answer this question, we must stop thinking of ourself as a separate individual, and begin thinking in terms of all of humanity—one spiritual unit within a much larger spiritual force. Once we do, we will begin to glimpse ways that the power of this noble purpose can enrich our own daily life.

The will to express the highest level of our wisdom and self-control, for instance, gives us enormous power to work continuously with excellence, even when we are pressured by time, weakened by illness, or distracted by temptations. The will to grow can give us the fortitude and stamina to endure moments of humiliation or defeat when we feel as though we have been abandoned by God and His whole Creation, as well as in many moments of lesser drama.

The development of the will as a parent provides an excellent example of this process. The first step lies in defining the responsibilities of parenting: to nurture and protect our children, physically and psychologically; to educate and inspire them to become mature adults; to guide them in their social and moral development; and to recognize and honor their temperament, strengths, and weaknesses.

The second step would be to make sure that our basic motive as a parent is one of goodwill—that we have an abiding faith in the emerging dignity and maturity of our children, plus a deep respect for their humanity, even as bratty little kids. This goodwill must be strong enough to temper our demands for obedience and our own irritability—even at times when our children defy or hurt us.

At this point, we are ready to consider the noble purpose of being a parent. What would be the ideal achievable outcome? Obviously, the answer to this would be happy, intelligent children who enter adulthood with good social skills, usable talents, and maturity. We can make this understanding even more powerful by putting it in the context of the archetypal: that society needs examples of inspired parenthood. It also needs the influx of young adults who have been brought up to realize their full potential, not spend their adult years trying to find it!

These connections with the purpose of parenting can give us the strength and fortitude to sustain ourself through all of the many daily challenges of being the best parent we can. It makes it easier to sacrifice our convenience for the good of our children; to resist peer pressure in holding our children to higher standards than other parents accept; and to greet the daily frustrations of being a parent with grace, cheerfulness, and a sense of gratitude.

The power of the will is tapped by regularly reaffirming our dedication to purpose. It builds gradually, through repetition—a repetition which may also serve to clarify and even amend some of our original insights into purpose. It is therefore important to keep an open mind, reviewing the progress we are making and setting the stage for new insights.

The education of the will requires a strong commitment to mature values. As we strive to develop the power of the will, this remarkable spiritual force will stimulate any pocket of personal stubbornness or rebellion that has not yet been redeemed.

So, we must take extra care to expand our goodwill, as well as more clearly define our enlightened values and convictions. We must also periodically ponder on the interconnectedness of all life—our shared responsibility for the growth and development of every facet of life that we touch—and to learn to put our emphasis on nurturing the potential for good in all things, not just condemn what is wrong.

True humility is another important safeguard in developing the will. The will tends to emphasize, at least at first, a powerful sense of egotism. For this reason, it is a good idea to remember always that there is a higher power—a cosmic power, in fact—to which we must answer and subordinate ourself. A dose of inspired humility and a regular practice of heartfelt piety and reverence will keep these temptations from getting out of line.

A simple exercise can help us examine our own use of the *will to grow*. This impulse to grow is a natural force deeply embedded in each of us.

We begin by defining our responsibility to grow in wisdom, virtue, skill, and usefulness. Are we pursuing this growth as a way of serving God—or because we hope to receive some personal gain, such as wealth, health, or security? How do we need to develop our character? What are the greatest lessons in our life? How would learning them help humanity as a whole as well as us personally? Would this growth be an individual experience—or one we could share with others?

Second, we need to assess our commitment to act with

goodwill. Do we believe that the will to grow leads us on a benevolent path, or that the effort to grow leads primarily to frustration and suffering? Do we spend most of our time fighting what is wrong with life—or are we primarily centered in building up what is right and good?

We should work on these first two steps until we have mastered them as completely as we can. Then, and only then, we should begin to define specific noble purposes in our life, by asking ourself:

How does God want me to grow?

What is the highest good I can achieve as I grow?

What is the best way to deal with irritability, anxiety, and depression?

How can I improve my ability to deal with loss, hardship, and opposition?

How can I approach my work with greater creativity and productivity?

How can I be more productive in spite of ongoing hardship, or even the apparent lack of opportunity?

In the process of answering these questions, we will begin to catch glimpses of the cosmic nature and purpose of growth, and tap the creative spiritual direction within our own life. As we then dedicate ourself to pursuing this growth, and consistently renew this dedication, we strengthen our use of spiritual will.

10.

Educating The Imagination

One of the most useful tools of personal growth is the human imagination. A fertile imagination enables us to take the first step out of the confines of the limited world of appearances, and begin working with the unlimited possibilities of universal life. A healthy imagination lets us speculate on and honor the ideals of life, even when we are mired in conditions that are anything but ideal. A strong imagination allows us to rehearse the best way of acting in a variety of circumstances, so that we can be ready to cope with whatever events come to us. An educated imagination lets us ponder on motives, trends, and purposes—the intangible forces of life. It also helps us focus on and relate to the good and noble elements within our friends and associates, rather than their petty or destructive traits.

Unfortunately, most of us have neglected to educate the

imagination so that it automatically performs these tasks. As a result, we often use the imagination like the way some people visit their local library. A library can be a tremendous asset to the learning process—if we know how to use it. But not everyone goes to the library to learn and to develop the mind. Some people stop by just to catch up on the latest Hollywood rumors—or pick up a romance novel. Others visit the video collection, but never the books. Some people just make it another stop in their daily routine, a chance to gossip—in whispers—with friends. For some, it is a quiet place to take a nap.

All too often, we interact with the imagination in much the same way. Instead of using the imagination as a tool of personal growth, we use it to stir up our wish life and fantasies—as a way to escape the dreary boredom of daily life. We pretend to be a movie star, a sports hero, or a charismatic leader. Or even worse, we harness the imagination to magnify our worries and fears, speculating on all the worst possibilities that could happen. We wonder, for example, what our friends really think of us, and start to conjure up all kinds of fears, from mild disapproval to outright condemnation and scorn. Sometimes, we go a step further, by speculating on the dark motives behind their words and actions. In this way, we sow seeds of distrust in our imagination, which grow rapidly into weeds that choke off wisdom and blur our perception of life.

Ideally, we would use a library to seek out and discover new ideas and understanding. In the same way, we are meant to learn to use the imagination as a staging ground where we can interact with the essence of good ideas, the higher nature of our friends and colleagues, the inner force of opportunities, and even elements of the sublime. But the ability to harness the imagination in this way does not come automatically. It must be learned. We must teach our imagination to search for the best within life, not be captured and dominated by the worst.

A healthy, educated imagination is a key element in our overall psychological well-being. It plays a vital role in the work of subduing the powerful forces of the innate urges and appetites of the personality. It is likewise a key to the process of transcending the physical plane. In the dense physical world, we are trapped in linear sequences—of both time and space. Once we do something in the physical plane, it becomes an integral part of our existence and character for the rest of our life. Just so, the linear future may seem fixed. But the imagination is not confined in this way. It can free us from this linearity, by letting us experiment with ideas and possibilities, projecting them into the future, rehearsing various options, and selecting the ideal choice.

Indeed, the imagination can even help us explore and understand that a specific event which has just occurred in the physical plane—a disaster, a disgrace, or a betrayal—may not be the monstrous, terrible thing we assume it to be. A well-trained imagination can help us find deeper meaning—and help us accept it—or create potential solutions that will let us turn the crisis into triumph, the disaster into progress.

If we visit a library but never check out anything except videos, we will miss the great storehouse of wisdom and ideas available to us there. We need to be trained to use the library more effectively.

Just so, most of us need to learn how to use the imagination effectively. The average person leaves the real potential of the imagination unexplored, untapped. Our traditional systems of education do almost nothing to address this problem or solve it.

As a result, until we decide to take on the challenge of educating ourself to the purpose and potential of the right use of the imagination, we are likely to misuse and abuse this great aspect of our consciousness.

Even worse, we may condemn ourselves to being trapped in a world of clichés and banalities—a world that is one-dimensional, dull, and literal.

Too many people poison the imagination by focusing it on the negative elements of their lives or environment. They harness the imagination to brood on the dark nature of their enemies, instead of using it to speculate on the potential to resolve the differences that exist between them. They obsess on the injury and terror of past miseries, reliving the pain and the horror time after time.

This act of focusing on the negative can sometimes be disguised as "important inquiry," as in the case of television and newspaper reporters dwelling constantly on reports of murder, rape, and automobile accidents. There is virtually no news substance in any of these stories, but they strike the morbid imagination of most viewers or readers, and so the same basic story is repeated to draw an audience.

The act of fundamentalist preachers condemning every-

127

one who disagrees with them as agents of the devil is a similar attempt to corrupt the imaginations of their followers with threats of divine rejection and punishment. They are doing nothing less than enticing the latent fear and guilt in these people, while addicting their imaginations to the need for more and more powerful "fixes" of the righteous conviction that their brand of religion will protect them from these threats.

Most of us, of course, pollute our imaginations all on our own. One of the most common ways we do this is by imagining "the worst case scenario" in a given set of circumstances, and then actually girding ourself for disaster. It can be helpful, on occasion, to speculate on the worst outcome of a chain of events, but only so we are prepared for all contingencies. When we visualize a worst case and then presume it will happen, however, we enter into the eerie twilight zone of self-fulfilling expectations.

Another common example of the power of a distorted imagination is the sex-mad teenager (or adult) whose fantasies and speculations are mostly X-rated. When such fantasies are permitted to control the imagination, they magnetically attract to a person coarse and grungy energies which abase, not elevate him or her.

The imagination can also be crushed by the dullness of a seemingly purposeless routine. This is not to suggest that any repeated activity is inherently dulling. But if an individual treats the chore or work to be done as drudgery, he generates an odd kind of self-absorption in the imagination that slowly shrinks the scope of his interests and activities, until he is virtually trapped in an earthbound shell.

The same impact on the imagination occurs when too much attention is devoted to petty, destructive activities— a constant obsession with video games, MTV, or what might be called "idiot TV"—as epitomized by daytime soap operas and talk shows.

We need to appreciate that the kind of forces we invite to direct and control our imagination will make a huge difference in every facet of our life. If we are undisciplined, then our sexual fantasies, wish life, worries and fears will mug us in the dark, take over control, and rule our life. These forces of the imagination will actually lead us magnetically toward certain kinds of experience (generally negative) and away from other types of experience (more spiritually rewarding).

But it need not be so. We can educate our imagination to become a constructive tool for speculating about the nature of life and for creating improvements in everything we do. We can train our imagination to become attuned to the higher possibilities and opportunites that lie before us. We can even learn to use the imagination to help us heal and bless others and life itself.

These are lessons each of us needs to master.

The basic lesson to be learned is easy enough: we must make sure that the very best within us, our highest good, is in charge of our imagination. If it is, then our speculations and inquiries into life will lead us repeatedly to the inner ideal, instead of the corruption and coarseness of the lower realms of human experience.

Take suspicion as an example—a word that originally

meant "to regard with awe, to look up to." Why do we suspect people of only corruption and mischief? Why not suspect them of honesty or courage or secret goodwill? The common variety of suspicion is a force that twists and distorts the human imagination. But the same kind of speculation could be focused toward the ideal qualities of human character just as easily as the crude and the base. We should become suspicious of light and love—meaning, of course, that we should look for them in everyone we meet. And why not?

The educated imagination is one that has been trained to respond primarily to the principles of right human living, not its problems. It reviews and reflects on our achievements, instead of brooding over our failures or difficulties. It magnifies our awareness of our strengths and talents, so that we exercise them fully, instead of obsessing about the blocks and barriers which impede us. It focuses us on what we like and can approve of in our friends and colleagues, in the events of life, and in our circumstances, as opposed to what we dislike and condemn.

In other words, we train the imagination by carefully and repeatedly focusing it on the good potential of all things—the force of meaning and noble purpose within our work, our relationships, the lessons we are learning, and much more. We may not be used to working with these higher possibilities, and so we may need to stretch our consciousness. This is where our imagination provides an indispensable service, by creating an attunement to the possibilities.

When most people come upon an obstacle in their progress—a fear of failure, for example—they eventually retreat, saying, "I can't do it." Usually, it is their own imagination that has fueled this belief. But they can learn to overcome this fear, by using the imagination more constructively—to focus on the opportunities before them. They can also use the imagination to defeat the fear, by recalling memories of overcoming similar obstacles in the past, and tapping the courage and strength which lies embedded in these memories.

As humans, we are not perfect. We have our share of difficulties. But the enlightened use of the imagination teaches us that there is something far more significant in life than our problems—namely, our inner strength and genius to overcome difficulty.

Some people believe their mission in life is somehow just to survive. This attitude is incredibly limiting. We are meant to confront our problems, learn from them, and prosper! To do so, however, we must have an active, well-focused imagination.

The work of educating the imagination takes us, eventually, into the realm of symbolic meanings and archetypal patterns. As this happens, we discover the great wellsprings of power and light available to us, for our work, our interactions with others, and much more. As we attune the imagination to our highest possibilities, we begin to cultivate a whole new perspective toward our self and life in general.

We begin to grasp the creative potential in our daily work—even if we had earlier viewed this work as dull and boring.

We begin to sense the depth of goodwill and support in the relationships we have nurtured.

We begin to embrace a broader sense of responsibility for our thoughts, our reactions, and our acts.

In this fashion, we learn to connect with the wellsprings of true power—the archetypal lights of divine life—and then use the imagination as an agent for making them a living presence within our consciousness. This power, love, and wisdom then become the basis for assessing our current and future challenges, a foundation for problem solving, and a keystone for producing a healthier self-image and self-expression.

It is this sort of intelligent exploration that propels us from the mundane to the sublime—from the earthbound to the spiritual. This is the esoteric work of the human imagination—to lead us out of the shadows into the light.

It is this light, of course, that is the inspiration for all personal creativity. A well-educated imagination is an indispensable part of all human creativity. It serves as the "docking mechanism" by which we hook up with glimmers of creative insight and bring them consciously into the workshop of the mind, creating new possibilities, solutions, and alternatives.

Having distilled the meaning of an event, for example, we can also use the imagination to conjure ways we can integrate this insight into our values and priorities, so that it becomes an active part of our daily life.

Two spiritual aspirants, for example, might suffer financial bankruptcy. The first might conclude that the life of spirit let him down when he most needed it, and turn his back on future spiritual growth. This individual has failed to use his imagination correctly—and, in fact, has let it be corrupted by the disappointment of his experience. The second, by contrast, uses his imagination to speculate on the meaning of his losses, and concludes that he has been learning to streamline his priorities and manage his resources more skillfully. This discovery of meaning becomes a liberating event for him, and allows him to plunge back into daily life with a fuller sense of who he is—and the way to success. He has used the imagination not only to understand the plans of the highest good within himself, but also to harness his highest possibilities.

Another good example of the creative value of the imagination would be the instance of a couple facing retirement. Instead of worrying about how they will survive, they harness the imagination to speculate on what they want to do with the rich years remaining to them. Where should they live? What resources will they need? What lessons ought they be learning? What contributions ought they be making? What kind of fulfillment do they seek?

There is no restriction on using the imagination for this type of expansion of meaning and understanding. The agent of light, for example, should make a regular practice out of redefining his or her relationship with God. This can be done by using the imagination to explore the answers and implications to a number of key questions:

What is the next step for me on the spiritual path?

What changes in my attitude, priorities, and lifestyle will be required to take this step?

What will happen if I do not make these changes?

How can I deepen my awareness of the presence of God in my life?

What lessons is life teaching me, and how can these lessons lead me closer to God?

What opportunities lie before me to use my talents to make a better contribution to the world?

One of the most effective ways to stimulate the imagination, of course, is to read a great work of fiction or mythology. It could be short, such as the parable of the Prodigal Son, or long, such as the *Odyssey* by Homer. It could have clear esoteric content, such as the Labors of Hercules, or it could be a good deal less obvious, such as the movie *Gremlins*. Or it could be any of a number of modern novels or plays: *Les Miserables*, *The Razor's Edge*, *The Good Earth*, or *The Crucible*. One of the richest sources of symbolism is modern science fiction and fantasy: *Star Wars*, Robert Heinlein's *The Glory Road*, Clifford Simak's *The Way Station*, or Colin Wilson's *The Philosopher's Stone*. The novels of Dave Duncan in particular create a rich tapestry of mythological meaning.

At first, the symbolic meaning of these stories may not be clear. This would be a sign that our imagination has not been highly stimulated or trained. So it is all the more important to resist the temptation to quit reading. Our imagination needs this kind of practice! It needs to be stretched and challenged; in particular, it needs to learn to leap up from the mundane to the spiritual.

Once we have become responsive to allegorical meanings in literature and films, then we need to put these insights to work in our own life. This does not occur by becoming an adventurer like Indiana Jones; it happens by translating the determination and one-pointedness he demonstrates into our own spiritual growth and daily activities.

Naturally, this type of work with allegory is not something we can do once and then forget; it must become an ongoing habit of inquiry. We must train ourselves to suspect the best within others—and to expect the best from life. Until we do, we will be using our imagination more to hold ourselves back—through worry, fear, and closed-mindedness—than to propel ourselves forward.

The agent of light must always make sure to approach life in forward gear.

11.

The Freedom To Learn

History is rife with examples of how learning is often stifled by society—or its institutions. The Catholic Church, in the Middle Ages, repressed the freedoms of discovery, invention, and creativity, frequently labeling scientists and other thinkers as "heretics." The result was to inhibit human learning and curiosity for centuries.

More recently, Adolph Hitler banned all kinds of books and persecuted any political or religious perspective that threatened his solidification of power in Germany. Under Marxism in the Soviet Union, Eastern Europe, and China, all religion was banned. And in modern Iran, death sentences were issued against Salman Rushdie, because he had the arrogance to write a book.

The most extreme portrayal of the repression of the freedom to learn and think can be found in George Orwell's chilling satire, *1984.* In this book, thought police snoop out and detect any citizens who may be inclined to harbor seditious, or even individualistic, thoughts. It represents the ultimate portrayal of our modern tendency to surrender individual freedoms "for the good of the state."

Of course, thought crimes do not yet exist officially in America, but they do exist unofficially, in the form of unspoken social sanctions which inhibit us from criticizing currently favored minorities, endorsing the need for moral fiber in our leaders, pointing out double standards in the press, or even discussing the need for personal responsibility in the conduct of life. The suggestion that the homeless or victims of abuse have a responsibility to straighten out their own lives, and not burden society with their troubles, is frequently drowned out by a long lecture about the need for "compassion."

Almost any mention of religion in public schools is now strictly prohibited, just as any discussion of psychic awareness and spirituality is taboo in psychology. Only recently has it become permissible to discuss prayer as an adjunct to physical medicine—but any health professional who dares bring up the subject still risks being ridiculed by his or her peers.

If a woman today were to paint in the style of Mary Cassatt, she would be condemned for perpetuating stereotypes of outmoded roles of women as mothers. In education, it has become a thought crime, routinely enforced by most colleges, to teach a curriculum based on DWEM—dead white European male thinkers and scientists.

In the arena of organized religion, any discussion of the

God within us sends many theologians and religionists into fits of hysteria. In the realm of holistic health, thought monitoring is practiced at both extremes—by medical doctors who decry any alternative approach to healing, and by holistic health fanatics who believe that only their herbs or techniques can do the job.

In some cases, the pressure to conform to acceptable thought patterns is a subtle one, voiced only in tones of disapproval from authorities and superiors. In other cases, however, it is blatant—as in denying a doctor his license to practice medicine.

Most people, of course, live out their lives without being touched by these threats. But those who have awakened from the slumber of the masses know them all too well. Their continued and future development of the mind and awareness is threatened by any restriction on the freedom to learn, whether the sanctions are official or merely informal.

Even worse, however, the whole of a culture becomes neurotic whenever the freedom to learn is limited or censored in any way. We need to understand that there is something seriously deficient in a society where:

· An educator who calls for greater personal responsibility is accused of blaming the victim for society's woes.

· A leader who calls for greater integrity is accused of being mean-spirited.

· An ordinary citizen who points out an obvious fault is accused of being judgmental.

· A person who extols excellence is accused of elitism.

The problem with censorship and thought control is that

it restricts the exercise of the mind to a narrow, closed box of homogenized, approved ideas. This is a terrible imposition on the human mind, which is designed to soar to transcendent heights, break down the limitations and barriers of the past, and explore every nook and crevice of life—even the dark corners filled with shadows. When limits are placed on our thinking, the mind is crippled, as though it were a hostage of terrorists, bound, gagged, and forced to lie in a four-by-six-foot cubicle. True learning becomes virtually impossible.

Learning still occurs, of course—but it is the wrong kind of learning. Under these limitations, the mind learns the lessons of intolerance, narrowmindedness, and laziness. We become either permissive and self-indulgent—or righteous and repressive. Discernment suffers, giving way to fantasies and wishes—or to arrogant fanaticism. Insight yields to opinion. Soon, our most cherished principles, values, and goals have been undermined.

Alexander Pope described an apocolyptic version of this threat in his mock epic poem, *The Dunciad*. As the poem ends, the goddess of Dullness has called on human vanity and bigotry to blot out all thinking and learning—in the sciences, the arts, and philosophy:

> No public flame, nor private, dares to shine;
> No human spark is left, nor glimpse divine!
> Lo! thy dread empire, Chaos! is restored;
> Light dies before thy uncreating word:
> Thy hand, great anarch! lets the curtain fall
> And universal darkness buries all.

139

When put in such dramatic terms, the threat seems distant and faraway. It is not. We need to open our eyes and see how commonly these boxes of thought regulation are placed on our own ideas and awareness. As thinking people, moreover, we need to do whatever lies in our power to smash every one of these boxes to splinters and shards.

We must understand our personal need to protect the freedom to learn for ourself, for our family—and for all of humanity.

There are seven boxes in which we may find ourselves trapped, if we allow cultural or social regulation to block our freedom to learn. Many of the ways in which these boxes entrap us are quite subtle and ingenious, so it is important to understand them thoroughly and make sure none is operative in our own mind and work.

The seven boxes that kill the freedom to learn are relativism, materialism, emotionalism, conformity, propaganda, paternalism, and genius envy. Each of these boxes represents a unique threat to the spirit of learning and discovery. It is important to learn to detect them, even in their subtle variations, and nurture the antidote which will protect us from succumbing to their noxious byproducts.

Let us therefore inspect these seven boxes more carefully:

Relativism is the concept that all truth is relative to the individual. Since no ultimate truth or authority exists—or so this box proclaims—we are free to believe whatever we want, and to change these beliefs at whim.

The danger of relativism is that it traps us in a subjective view of life, and alienates us from the universal principles that govern all of life's activities. When we fall into this trap, our life becomes empty, devoid of significance. We begin to believe that human life is just an accident of random chance and is supported by no inner core of intelligence. The logical extension of this concept is that learning becomes nothing more than the quest for some thin, superficial advantage over others, as opposed to a steady evolution toward the realization that life has a meaning and purpose greater than our personal experience.

In the box of relativism, there are no facts—just opinions. There is no right or wrong—just what we want to believe at the moment. We develop the bizarre idea that reality exists only within our personal mind; therefore, whatever we think or believe is "real."

Is anyone trapped in this box? Most of American society is, to one degree or another. This is why we are suffering through an era in which everyone is obsessed with their rights as a citizen, while turning blind eyes to the meaning of personal responsibility. The problem is that the term "rights" has lost almost all of its meaning in recent years, as it is applied to everything from leading a homosexual lifestyle to the desire to be excused for criminal acts. It is as though these people are saying, "Society owes me my special indulgence; I owe it nothing." It is about as logical as the philanderer who protests: "I don't have a mistress, and she's not a blonde."

Our protection against being trapped in the box of relativism is to realize that the world is bigger than we are. It has also been here a lot longer than we have, and will still be here long after we depart. We had better open our eyes and study the ways life operates, conforming to its principles, rather than trying to make it conform to our wishes. There is an indwelling intelligence and truth in life; learning occurs as we discover it and apply it to our own self-expression.

Just as driving the wrong way down a one-way street leads ultimately to a heavy penalty, there are rules to life. These rules or principles cannot be neutralized by either denial, bribery, or self-deception. The highest act of intelligence is to seek to understand these laws—and then to conform our life to them.

Materialism is the ardent belief that the only realities of life are those we can see, touch, hear, or measure physically. Abstractions, the materialist claims, exist only within the human mind and imagination. As a result, in the box of materialism, physical objects and energies are the only realities we are allowed to consider, and the solution to all problems must be found in the physical plane. All diseases, even psychological ones, must have physical causes—and cures. All social problems, such as poverty or crime, must have physical origins. Unspoken thoughts and feelings are irrelevant and therefore harmless. Genius and creativity are mere flukes of some abnormality in brain chemistry—as are happiness and peace. In this particular box, the quality of life can only be measured tangibly—e.g., by the size of our bank account.

The flaw in materialism, quite obviously, is that it ignores and denies the influence of spirit and the archetypal forces of life. These are always the true source of genius and creativity, of contentment and peace. Materialism severs its adherents from higher sources of guidance and joy, blinding them to the true causal forces of life.

Since the materialist believes, for instance, that all problems have physical causes, the act of learning is reduced to a mechanical process that leads to the manipulation of behavior and social conditions, rather than the growth of maturity and responsibility. The materialist assumes that thinking occurs in the brain, not the mind, and thereby trivializes the nature of character, intelligence, and spirit. As a result, tragic missteps have occurred in the recent development of psychotherapeutic methods, as well as in public education.

The antidote to being trapped by this box is to learn to look beyond superficial appearances. Just as we have to learn to look beyond the wit, drama, and violence to tap the symbolic meaning of a book or movie, we need to train ourselves to look beyond the physical level of life to discover the true causes of anything. We need to trace in our mind the relationship between the physical events of life and the inner forces and factors that shape them.

Because our thoughts and intentions are relevant to every phase of human activity and learning, they need to be given greater weight in our assessments of life than materialistic factors. As long as we are trapped in materialism, we can never understand the true causes of life.

Emotionalism is the condition in which a person or group of people makes decisions based on wishes, doubts, anger, guilt, or fear, rather than an intelligent understanding of the issues. This particular box often leads to stereotyping of others and life, plus an emotional attachment to the status quo. Opinions are readily substituted for facts and knowledge. Emotionalists prefer flattery to the truth, and value charm over character. They make choices that appease the emotions, and then use the mind—if the mind is operating at all—to rationalize their choice.

This is not genuine thinking! It makes the mind a slave to the emotions. The grave danger in emotionalism is that the truth becomes an enemy to our belief structure whenever it fails to flatter us. The emotionalist is forced to live a lie; his whole view of life is conceived and nurtured in a state of intellectual dishonesty. Such a person is easily snared by fads, sensationalism, and defensiveness. Overblown, hysterical images of life become a standard. The emotionalist cannot take criticism, cannot bear the burden of his or her own flaws.

The overwhelming majority of human beings are trapped in the box of emotionalism, to a greater or lesser degree. This encumbrance is reflected in the media's fascination with scandal and conflict and the outrageous exploitation of human misery by talk shows. Almost every "principle" of advertising is based on the persuasive power of emotionalism. But the threat of emotionalism to the freedom to learn becomes much clearer when we see how it is used by demagogues to stir up the passion of supporters. Everyone would like to see hunger eliminated, for example; the demagogues of starvation use this sympathy to drum up donations to feed themselves. The same pattern is repeated among environmental extremists. Everyone wants to see pollution reduced; the green demagogues, however, play on this natural desire to promote programs to destroy industry, overthrow capitalism, and misinform the public for their own advantage.

The cure for emotionalism is to give priority to thinking, rather than feeling. We must learn to make decisions based on our values, goals, and principles—not just what feels right. An important first step toward implementing this cure is to train ourself always to focus on common sense ideas and solutions that will improve life, not just make us feel good.

Conformity is a box that begins trapping people when they are teenagers and never lets them go. It is a horrendous blight on thinking, and almost as common as emotionalism. It represents a surrender to group attitudes and current fads—a willingness to go with the flow, out of fear of disapproval.

The danger of conformity, of course, is that it inhibits our native intelligence and ability to think for ourself, and replaces it with a dull, robotic imitation of what others think and do. It short circuits understanding by equating truth with what a majority of people believe. Our thinking therefore becomes more responsive to peer pressure than to the light of intelligence.

A common example of this box would be the journalist who writes for professional recognition instead of public enlightenment. A second example would be the intense pressures on the modern woman to pursue a career rather than motherhood in order to find fulfillment as a person. A third would be the popular notion that big government is wonderful but that big business is always evil.

145

To combat this box of conformity, we must reject the assumption that whatever is popular is good. Peer pressure or conformity is probably the most seductive corruption of thinking, because it ignores the uniqueness of any given situation in favor of an all-purpose interpretation. But conformity is not an easy box to break out of, because it is subtly reinforced by psychic pressures and expectations from mass consciousness. We must therefore train ourselves to see the uniqueness within other people and events, striving always to develop individual solutions and plans, not "cookie cutter" concoctions. We also need to learn to evaluate the results of actions we take, and be ready to modify our plans if they are not helping us meet our goal. The need to pay attention to feedback in this way is illustrated by the failure of some Marxist intellectuals to admit the demonstrated ineffectivenesss of communism as a form of government.

Ultimately, the best way to defeat the pressure to conform is to dedicate ourselves to discerning and honoring the highest good within ourselves, others, situations, and society. This effort must become more important to us than the desire to please others—or submit to what others expect.

Propaganda is a most pernicious box, in that its chief use is to persuade people to do things against their best interests. The only way it can succeed, of course, is if we allow our mind to be brainwashed.

Successful propaganda does not always involve outright lying, but it always involves the basic premise of persuading people to believe or accept things they would otherwise ignore or reject. It is a common part of almost all modern advertising, and is frequently a part of political campaigns. Ninety percent of the news we read and hear is propaganda, rather than news. So is the bulk of what we hear from the pulpit—and one hundred percent of what we hear from "spin doctors."

What is the difference between legitimate news and propaganda? The news is a statement of facts, as they have been observed and gathered. Propaganda is the use of these same facts (or lies) to seduce a person or group into embracing a specific, prepackaged conclusion—not by asking that they make up their own mind, but by forcibly persuading them. The key word is "persuade"—changing their minds to conform with the desired opinion or proposal.

The grave danger of propaganda is that its targets often end up brainwashed, accepting beliefs, doing things, or buying products they would otherwise ignore. They are maliciously and intentionally led down a carefully etched path to false conclusions, until their own thinking ends up in step with those who are manipulating them. In this way, their higher intelligence is deliberately suppressed.

A good example of propaganda is the prevalent use of statistics to "prove" the existence of racial or sexual discrimination. We are told that the reason why so many members of certain racial groups cannot graduate from high school is because they do not receive an equal education, owing to past or present discrimination. They therefore need special treatment in order to succeed. What is being overlooked is the fact that record numbers of these groups are indeed graduating from high school and attending college. If these people can do it, how is discrimination barring the efforts of their fellow students? The answer, of course, is that it is not.

University students are also prime targets of brainwashing, as contradictory as that seems at first. Instead of teaching college students to think, our colleges teach them political correctness, economic bias, and moral blindness. They are routinely taught, for example, that Marxism is a viable system and that it is capitalism which is failing, not the reverse!

The antidote to propaganda is simplicity itself: deliberate and careful thinking. Instead of rushing to judgment and premature conclusions about any issue, we must learn to prolong our evaluation of new ideas and reports until we can get all sides of the story and collect all relevant facts. We need to learn to look for and spot the hidden agendas and devious motives of those who deliver "the news," and discount the authenticity of those who have misled us in the past. We must be alert for inconsistences and discrepancies—and try always to place what we are told into the context of what we have already tested and proven to be true.

Genius envy is the modern tendency to be jealous of success in any form, especially if it represents a triumph of individuality. It is an odd byproduct of the unaccountable popularity of Marxism among many segments of American society. Simply put, it regards excellence, achievement, and genius as "elitist"—and, therefore, an insult to the average person. Genius envy is a social movement that seeks to "level the playing field" by making mediocrity the pinnacle of aspiration. It is dangerous because it has its roots in attitudes as seemingly innocent as the American love for the underdog, which has subtly taught most of the nation to distrust—if not openly hate—the high achiever.

The danger in the box of genius envy is that merit and achievement cease to be goals or ideals in our society. In fact, the "high achiever" is now being held up as a negative example—someone who works too hard, demands too much from others, and injures the self-esteem of those who cannot do as well. As such, genius envy has become the single most damaging force inhibiting the process of learning today. It suppresses curiosity and undermines self-reliance.

Examples of genius envy abound, from the scorn with which the typical high school student views achievement to the dumbing down of the curricula at every level of education. In addition to academic standards that fall more rapidly than prices at Wal-Mart, genius envy can be seen in the championing of crude, vulgar forms of music, art, and literature at the expense of others with obvious merit. It can also be found in the blatant intimidation of workers in any bureaucracy to lower their productivity and standards— and for the increasing tendency in public education to ignore incompetence in teachers and aides.

The antidote to genius envy begins with our personal attitudes. We must make sure that we respect genius, hard work, and excellence, striving for them in all that we do. We must learn to take pride in and find joy in outstanding accomplishments, and not indulge the immaturity of friends or associates who would put down the value of achievement. In addition, we should do all that we can

149

to promote maturity over immaturity—in literature, music, the arts, and social debate.

These seven boxes should be thought of as diseases of the mind—deadly diseases that are highly infectious. We are exposed to them every day, at work, on television, and in every public forum. In fact, they are so common it is easy to ignore them. Yet the moment they take hold on our thinking, they strip away a major portion of our freedom to learn. We become trapped in our "own ideas."

It is therefore important to do whatever is necessary to break free from these boxes. We must reclaim the territory of our mind, and reassert our mental independence and freedom.

Until we heal our own thinking, we cannot hope to heal the larger problems in society.

The road to reclaiming our freedom to learn is the same as it is with any kind of freedom: *We must exercise vigilance.*

We must examine our attitudes, assumptions, priorities, and actions as we go through each day. Are we ever caught in one of these traps? How do we avoid being trapped in one of these seven boxes? How do we free ourself once we end up in one?

As an exercise in mental vigilance, we can pick any one of the seven boxes and work on it in our reflections or meditations, asking:

When did we become trapped in this particular box? How did it happen? How did it interfere with our efforts to grow and learn? Have we been able to free ourself from the box—or are we still trapped?

If we are still trapped, have we made an effort to get a greater understanding of this situation? Are we in denial that we caused this mess ourself? Have we set goals and standards? What are they? Are we stereotyping? Are we afraid to risk disapproval?

If we have freed ourself from the trap, what have we learned from this experience? How do we now make crucial decisions? Are we able to choose between being popular and being correct? Are we able to choose between denying a problem exists and confronting the truth? Are we able to choose between what we feel to be right and what we value?

What is our yardstick for measuring effectiveness?

What does it mean to make a commitment to think— and, even more importantly—to think for ourself?

As we gather insights and facts through these reviews, we must be sure to check the reality of our conclusions. If we adopt new methods to correct a problem, do they actually make our situation better—or does the act of trying just give us a comfortable feeling?

The purpose of this exercise is not to indulge in self-deception—by deciding that we are doing everything we can. Quite the reverse, our goal is to clarify our thinking, so that we are not unknowingly trapped in any of the seven boxes that will prevent us from learning.

The freedom to think and learn is a freedom that no government or declaration can guarantee for us. We must guarantee it for ourself.

12.

Our Responsibility To Learn

The opportunity to learn is one of the great privileges of human living; it is the doorway through which we discover our birthright of the light within us. But the presence of an opportunity to learn does not guarantee that we actually will respond to it.

Even being placed in a traditional learning environment is no guarantee that learning will happen. Millions of kids sit in schools throughout the world daily without ever learning to think. They may pass exams, be politically correct, and even have a high self-esteem, but they nonetheless fail to become self-initiating learners.

Just so, as adults, we regularly face challenging learning situations, at work, in our relationships, and in response to our duties. But do we learn anything of value to the higher self as a result—or do we just find a way to survive? All too frequently, the only "learning" that occurs teaches us all the wrong lessons—to shift responsibility to others, to reinforce our prejudices, and to get our way by manipulation. Unfortunately, these particular lessons obscure the gentle encouragement of the higher self to grow—to focus our mind and curiosity to grasp our potential for new understanding, love, and resourcefulness.

To be an agent of light, we need to appreciate the immense difference between the process of learning and the mere absorption of facts and knowledge. The learning process often begins with the collection of facts, but it must take us far beyond this first phase in order to produce true learning. Once we have gathered relevant facts, we must distill their meaning and translate it into new understanding, producing a level of insight that provides a glimpse of the design of the higher self. We must then integrate the power of this insight into our sense of purpose and values, and then into our attitudes and habits. Only when the whole process has been completed can we truly state that we have learned something of value.

This act of learning can only occur within us, as a result of our own initiative. It cannot be imposed on us, either by a teacher, a parent, or a government. Teachers and parents may play a crucial role in inspiring us to want to learn, but only we can make the process happen. The work of learning therefore requires a strong and steady commitment—a sense of duty to learn every lesson that life undertakes to teach us.

In the adventure of life, new opportunities to learn confront us daily. It is not necessary to be in a school or college in order to learn. Schools can help, but the real value of formal education is to demonstrate how learning occurs. Once we have mastered this lesson, learning is meant to become an individual pursuit—an individual responsibility.

To live up to our full potential as an agent of light, there are four basic ways we need to seize responsibility for learning. First, we must eliminate any barriers to learning within ourselves that would keep us from learning—or trying. Second, we must cultivate specific skills in thinking and integration that will enhance the learning process, allowing it to proceed more rapidly and less painfully. Third, we must learn to probe into the inner levels of meaning and abstraction—the essence of ideas. And fourth, we must cultivate the ability to discern what is useful to us—and what needs to be left behind.

The easiest way to sabotage the learning process is to overlook or discount the barriers of attitude that undermine our capacity to learn. The most common of these barriers can also be the most subtle—the arrogant belief that we know enough to get by in life. We know enough to get by at work. We know enough to have opinions about public life. We know enough to raise kids. We know enough to be a helpful spouse. Why learn anything more?

The answer, of course, is that we can never know too much about life. Our daily chores may be limited, but our opportunity to express joy, love, wisdom, and peace through them is limitless. There is never any valid reason to stop learning.

A similar barrier is the notion that we are too busy to take the time to learn. We are already so productive and efficient that there is no time left to study, learn, or grow. This attitude overlooks the fact that the time invested in learning is always repaid with interest. It also fails to understand that the need for efficiency is another quality that expands with the task; no matter how proficient we may be, the moment we become complacent, we cease being as efficient as we might become.

A third barrier to learning is intellectual defensiveness. Having carefully built a small but comforting set of core beliefs, we view all new or different ideas with suspicion, instead of the more desirable spirit of discovery. As a result, all new ideas are rejected as heretical or dangerous, and the scope of our mental explorations remains shrunken and insignificant.

This is always the problem of the fundamentalist (in any field), who assumes the pompous attitude: "I am the center of the known universe; what I know is all there is. Whatever I do not know is either irrelevant or unknowable."

Perhaps the saddest barrier of all, though, is the nihilistic belief that we have no lessons to learn in life. Whatever is wrong about life is simply someone else's fault—or society's. Instead of learning, we opt for the course of suffering and bitching. We focus entirely on the problem, rather than a solution, thereby preserving the problem. In this way, we start out by learning the wrong lesson—that life has no meaning—and continue to repeat it until we become exhausted by our own circular logic.

How do we eliminate these barriers? We must challenge

the assumptions which led to these attitudes, and disengage their power over our thinking. In their place, we must build a strong conviction that our life is an adventure in learning. Every day brings us a new set of experiences, each experience containing a "message" that can help us grow.

Some people visit museums as if it were a test to see how quickly they can reach the finish line. The more thoughtful individual, however, sets a slower pace, seeking to interact fully with the art—and the intelligence and beauty behind it. This thoughtfulness requires a number of educated skills. We must be able to perceive what is actually on the canvas—the light and shadow, texture, color, and form which constitute the style of the artist. In addition, we must examine what mood this painting strikes within us. Does it inspire us, depress us, trouble us, or lift us up to angelic realms? What is the symbolic meaning of specific parts? What does the picture as a whole say to us? We might also find it helpful to compare the painting to other works by the same artist, and others who worked in the same genre.

Sometimes, we react to a painting with dislike. If it is just bad art, the reaction is appropriate. But if it is actually good art that we do not understand, then we should see this painting or artist as a lesson waiting to be learned. We need to broaden our perceptiveness and comprehension.

In much the same way, the art of learning demands that we cultivate certain appropriate skills. To begin with, we need to learn to observe life and ideas from more than one perspective—i.e., our own. If something unpleasant happens to us, for example, we should not automatically assume that we are a victim. Perhaps we are getting exactly what we deserve. Or perhaps it is our own egotistical demands that have caused this unpleasantness. It therefore could be a wonderful opportunity to learn. We will never know—unless we look at the situation from every possible perspective.

A second valuable skill in pursuing the art of learning is the ability to interpret the meaning of details and our overall experience. As we encounter a life situation, for example, it can be useful to compare it to similar experiences in our past. As a pattern emerges, we should ask: what lesson am I persistently overlooking? How can I free myself from this pattern?

A related skill involves the ability to find the symbolic meanings in the events of life. To some people, symbolism is a foreign language; their blindness causes them to miss a great deal of insight. They need to learn that symbolism is a primary way to discover the underlying meaning of seemingly irrelevant events or conditions. The inability of a friend to help us at a time of great need might, for example, be a symbol of our own unwillingness to help others unless it serves to advance our own agenda.

One of the best ways to trigger new insight into what we need to learn about any situation is to examine what chord this experience strikes within us. Is it guilt, fear, or doubt? Or just indifference? Perhaps it is excitement, hope, or aspiration. Why are we reacting in this way? Is this reaction a valid response to the event—or is there a higher, more enlightened perspective we should be cultivating?

In general, if any situation "tears us apart" emotionally, it should be seen as a sign that we were not very well put together emotionally in the first place. We need to cultivate a stronger mental focus that would let us meet this situation with confidence, clarity, and competence.

It can also be helpful to compare our actions to known patterns or templates, either in our own experience or in the experiences of others. If we have not had much experience in forgiving the offenses of others, for example, it may be useful to review the life of someone who has embodied the spirit of forgiveness—or even read a novel that lucidly dramatizes it.

Finally, we should also cultivate the excellent habit of asking one basic question about every major lesson of life: what is the real question this event is asking us? Instead of asking, "What is wrong with our childhood?" or "What is wrong with society?" we need to ask, "What is wrong within us? What changes must we make? What new steps must we embark upon?"

Just cultivating the skill to examine the events of life in this manner is not enough, however. We must also learn to probe more completely the inner levels of meaning.

Every facet of physical life is full of rich levels of inner significance—but the meaning is not always apparent physically. In fact, this inner meaning is often quite different from the obvious or superficial significance of the outer event. A diagnosis of cancer, for example, would be distressing news to most people, but the experience of healing this disease may well turn out to be anything but tragic. The treatment may involve hardship and suffering, to be sure—but it may also produce many desirable changes in our lifestyle. We may decide to stop being a workaholic, we may rediscover the love and support of family members, and we may even build a greater attunement to spirit.

Because the inner meaning can be obscure, we must learn to look for it in every facet of our life, and we must be sure to look in the right places—in the abstract regions of the higher self, not in our wishes or emotional reactions.

Just what is meaning? It is the implication, momentum, consequence, and larger purpose of an event, as it appears to the inquiring mind. In other words, the meaning to us of contracting a life-threatening disease is that we should have begun taking steps to protect our health many years ago—and now must accelerate the process.

Why is meaning important to learning? It is through the discovery of meaning that we are able to extract wisdom from our experiences—to find value in our suffering. This wisdom greatly intensifies the pace of learning for us—we become more perceptive, persistent, and discerning. It also helps us see other implications in the lessons we are learning.

All experiences in life have meaning and value, because we can learn from every type of event. The mastery of this process of extracting meaning from the events of life helps us achieve a more refined level of learning, where it becomes possible to glimpse the hand of God at work in our life. We begin to understand archetypal force, divine principles, and cosmic laws—*as they apply to our life!*

This contact with divine life is our ultimate heritage as an agent of light.

The fourth responsibility we bear for making the learning process work for ourself is to recognize what is useful—and to reject what is not. We are bombarded daily by huge masses of information and ideas, from the media, teachers, friends, and the feedback of our own efforts. Some of this input may well be helpful and should be registered. Some, by the same token, is clearly harmful and needs to be rejected. The rest is just irrelevant.

Part of this process of evaluation needs to include a review of ideas and interpretations made by us in the past, to insure that our conclusions are still relevant and helpful. A few erroneous conclusions about being victimized as a child, for example, can keep us from learning the genuine lessons of adulthood.

It is our responsibility to evaluate whatever information comes to us, to determine what to do with it. Is it accurate and helpful? Is it a balanced view—or is it biased? Is it based on fact—or just gossip and rumor? If it is factual, does it lead us to a valuable inner meaning—or is it potentially misleading and corrupting? If useful, how best can we put it to work in our life? Is it helpful right now—or is it something to store away for later use?

This is not a theoretical exercise. As in school, every lesson we learn ends with a test. We have to apply what we have learned and judge for ourself whether or not it is useful. The test is not designed to judge us, but to encourage us to experiment with new ideas and possibilities—and make revisions as necessary. The response of life itself to our effort to learn becomes the basis for evaluating our own progress.

The central work of any learning process is to practice the skill we wish to acquire. A simple exercise to strengthen our responsibility for learning from life is to take time at the end of each week to review a basic question:

"What have we learned this week?" The answer might lie in our work, character, relationships, or spiritual growth.

This primary question should be followed by four others:

"What inner barriers have sabotaged us—blind spots, areas of resistance, defensiveness, or cherished assumptions? Where did our thinking become trapped in a concrete or one-sided perspective?"

"What patterns of new understanding are emerging as we work with this lesson?"

"What is the message within these patterns?

"How can we integrate this lesson into our beliefs and behavior?"

Answering these questions week after week will quickly attune us to our responsibility to learn. Learning is a challenge—an invitation from the higher self to rise up and join it at a more dynamic level of living. It is a challenge we cannot afford to miss. We must respond!

13.

Using What We Learn

The effort to learn anything is pointless, unless it leads to greater knowledge and skill—increased maturity as a human being, expanded wisdom as a thinker, or refined creative talents. There is a subtle reason why this is so. It is tempting to think that a lesson is learned once we have understood what the problem is. But the process of learning is far more complex. In addition to the problem, each lesson we encounter contains a larger meaning—the true solution—as well as the need to act. Until we learn to embrace all three elements, the "lessons" we learn will be strangely ineffective and superficial.

There is no question but that insight into our problems arrives first, and often impresses us as being all there is to know. After all, this core idea frequently brings with it an explanation of a major mystery that has puzzled us for years.

We are therefore not inclined to look beyond this initial wave of insight. We are more than satisfied with what we have learned. But we should not be. We are still missing the major parts of the remedy.

Perhaps we have finally gained insight into our anger, after many years of alienating friends and family. This is a great step forward, but there are still two fundamental aspects of the lesson to be added:

1. We must learn how to manage our anger, not just explain it. We must learn that anger can only be dissolved by mastering the expression of goodwill.

2. We must do it! We must learn that one of the active expressions of goodwill is forgiveness. Until we have thoroughly mastered the ability to apply goodwill through forgiveness of those who have hurt us, past, present, and future, we actually know very little about anger management and control.

Learning, in other words, does not stop with the identification of a specific lesson or skill that we need. It continues well after the message begins to dawn in our awareness. It forces us to take the message we have acquired and transmute it into wisdom—and then apply this wisdom in practical, effective ways in daily living.

In short, we need to take the new insights and skills we are learning out for a test drive and see how they handle. If we end up crashing, we will know that our understanding was not as complete as we had imagined. The problem may lie in our own limited understanding—or it may be a limitation of the message itself.

One of the problems that besets certain self-absorbed

people is that they are boring. They do not know how to listen to friends or relate their own ideas to others with enough elán and charm to interest or amuse them. As a result, they become estranged from effective interaction with others, making the problem worse.

It would be quite a revelation for such a person to discover that all he needs is to take a vital interest in the affairs and needs of others. But there is a huge gap between the concept of what is needed and the effective expression of it in the company of others. Before the solution to his problem becomes active in his own life, he must figure out how to break down the walls of his self-absorption, as well as learn to respect his family and friends as actual people, not chess pieces to move about or manipulate.

The need to apply the lessons of life we have learned is a vital part of the educational process. We create an illusion of learning in school, by absorbing an enormous number of facts. But nothing of value is actually learned until we take these facts, convert them into wisdom and skill, and then find a way to put them to work in our life.

On the spiritual path, the agent of light is primarily interested in the lessons of spiritual maturity. We seek to learn to express patience, courage, self-discipline, cheerfulness, tolerance, and persistence, as well as social skills, leadership skills, and the ability to handle and manage conflict. With the right tools, it becomes relatively easy to gain the insight we need. What takes time is the trial and error process of testing the insights we have gained, and then integrating them into our character and self-expression, once we are sure we have learned the right lesson.

Some people, of course, are not motivated to learn these lessons thoroughly. They prefer to bluff their way along the spiritual path. But as Alexander Pope warned us, a little learning is a very dangerous thing. Half an answer can be far more troublesome than no answer at all.

We need to understand that higher intelligence is truly intelligent. Unless we learn to use the lessons and insights that have already been given to us, no more will be made available. The result will be a clogging of consciousness, creating an odd kind of stagnation which is the equivalent of mental indigestion. We may become stuck in a morass of procrastination, a limbo of infinite possibilities and limited opportunities.

In such an event, all forward progress must halt, until we liberate ourself from the rut.

Our great need in every learning situation is to stay connected to the impelling spiritual message of the lesson, and the larger context in which it exists. We must resist the temptation to adopt only superficial changes, without touching the substance of new maturity.

The classic example of the person who touches the appearance of a lesson, yet fails to embrace its life force or larger meaning, is the college professor who collects a library full of theories and speculations about his or her specialty, yet never applies these ideas in any constructive way. To such a person, it is the concept that counts, not its practical application. In the pursuit of light, however, this way of thinking must be redirected. The agent of light is primarily interested in putting ideas to work for humanity.

In the realm of personal growth, the equivalent of the ivory tower professor would be the aspirant who discovers a personal flaw or weakness, then spends the rest of his or her life justifying it rather than reforming it. Millions of Americans are discovering that they have been a victim in one way or another in their lives—and then fail to accept the challenge to stop being victimized! They fail to cultivate the spiritual qualities of courage and strength and goodwill that would let them stand up to bosses and family members who exploit or manipulate them. Insight into their problems simply makes them "happy" in their misery—it does not complete the lesson. Only when they learn that life does not support victimization will they be able to tap the ideal's inner power that will liberate them.

In esoteric circles, the problem of learning incompletely can be even more disastrous. Learning about kundalini and permanent atoms and chakras can easily engender the illusion of rapid spiritual growth, yet trap the aspirant in a labyrinth of his or her own construction—a maze of knowledge and facts that eclipses the light of spirit. Esoteric information is relatively useless, as long as it remains unused—and potentially dangerous, if abused. It is meant to be taken by each aspirant and translated into meaningful daily expressions that help others, enrich life in general, and reconcile inner divisions.

An obvious example of this would be those astrological students who believe that their character is largely determined by the stars. Instead of using this information to make intelligent improvements in their character, they accept who they are as a matter of fate. This attitude creates a variety of passiveness that negates much of the usefulness of the personality to the soul.

The notion that "learning for learning's sake" is the most noble form of learning is misguided, empty, and vacuous. Life becomes a theoretical game played by theoretical contestants from the secure distance of the ivory tower. To borrow from computer lingo, the end result might aptly be called "virtual reality." It looks real, it feels real, but it is not.

The true lessons of life do not separate us from the primary flow of events. They do not isolate us. Quite the contrary, they involve us even more deeply in our duties, our creative challenges, and our opportunities to serve. A lesson in living fully learned does three things:

1. It reveals our goal.
2. It shows us how to proceed.
3. It impels us on our way.

Ultimately, we must learn to reverse our perspective on learning. We tend to think that a lesson is something that is going to enrich our abilities and transform our capacity to act. The emphasis is placed clearly on the personality and how it will be helped. As a result, the attitude of the personality toward learning becomes a primary factor in determining how much is learned.

Eventually, the agent of light begins to realize that it is the soul that benefits the most from the lessons the personality is learning, because these lessons allow the soul to gain greater and more complete use of the personality!

167

This is how it works: as the personality is struggling to become more patient, so that it will not be so upset by the irritating forces of life, the soul is simultaneously learning to use the personality to express more divine peace on the earth plane. As the personality struggles to overcome anger and replace it with forgiveness, the soul is learning to use its personality to express more of the goodwill of spirit.

To the individual bogged down in victimhood, it may seem remote that the real lesson to be learned is accountability and self-reliance, but it is. And unless we learn the knack of looking for and finding the larger context in which our problems are occurring, we will never find the clues that help us fully solve them.

This is a crucial point to understand: real learning leads to the appearance of better character skills and qualities in our daily life—or the emergence of new talents. Personal growth does not occur simply by becoming a more efficient neurotic or a better manipulator of those around us. It does not occur by withdrawing from life—or by denying responsibility for our acts and attitudes. On the contrary, real growth should steadily reveal to us the benevolent guidance of our higher intelligence, as it leads us through the lessons we need to be an active, skilled, and intelligent adult.

Naturally, these lessons vary for each person. This is the principle of individuality at work. But the purpose behind this growth does not vary; it is the same for us all. We are designed to discover the impulse to grow within us and learn to cooperate intelligently with it. Learning is one of the most human things we can do.

But what if we discover, at age fifty, that we have failed

to use the lessons of life in this way? Are the past thirty years of adulthood a waste? Not at all. We still retain the ability to learn from the lessons of these thirty years—all fifty of them, in fact—even though we have left some or all of them incomplete.

The first step to take, at whatever age we begin this process, is to review the pattern of our life's lessons. Problems do not come to us randomly; they come to us in patterns. As we examine these patterns, we can discover the clues we need in order to understand the major spiritual purposes they serve.

In examining our experiences in this way, we must remember that the personality defines problems differently than the soul. What the personality calls "irritation" the soul is likely to view as "resistance to truth." What the personality sees as "righteous anger" the soul is apt to view as "childish hostility." The more we can view the patterns of our learning from the perspective of the soul, the more quickly we will accurately discern the spiritual lessons we are striving to master.

Most of these patterns will be painfully active in the present, defining the major traumas we are presently struggling to overcome. It will therefore be in the present that we first discover the power to act with the life force of a particular lesson—as we harness the spiritual will of the soul to neutralize the irritation of the personality, or as we invoke the goodwill of the soul to transform our current anger into forgiveness and helpfulness. But only a portion of the work will actually be focused on the present. A large amount must be focused on the past, as we go back in our memories and heal the beliefs and reactive patterns associated with similar difficulties from many years ago—even childhood.

Obviously, we can no longer act with courage or goodwill in an event that happened twenty years ago; our time to act has passed. But we do have the opportunity to reenact the situation mentally, this time behaving in a mature, spiritual way, instead of immaturely. In this way, we retrain the subconscious to learn the habit of maturity, instead of repeating the automatic behavior of immaturity.

This reenactment does not in any way represent a repression or denial of the past. We retain full conscious memory of these events—but with a difference. Instead of associating the event from the past with failure and disgrace, we now associate it with growth and wisdom, because we have acted upon the lesson we finally learned!

In this regard, it is also important to remain vigilant in our application of any lesson we learn. We may have buried some childhood experiences of this pattern quite deeply, in unconscious layers of awareness. These memories may suddenly arise into our conscious awareness, when we least expect them. Unless we are prepared to meet them as another phase of the learning process, they may take us by surprise and cause us to think that we have not learned our lesson after all. In fact, it is just another chapter in a very long process.

It is also important to remember what our true goal is. It is not to become less neurotic or less angry or less withdrawn. These are defensive maneuvers that postpone learning. Our true goal is to become more mature—more enlightened. Our true goal is to become an agent of light, enabling the soul within us to use our personality to express all manner of spiritual qualities and skills.

For this reason, it is not enough just to act wisely in the present and reform the past. Consciousness extends forward as well as backward, and we are just as motivated by our values, our sense of identity, and our priorities as we are by unredeemed issues from the past. So we must examine these factors as well, to see how this new measure of goodwill or patience or joy can be integrated into our values, our priorities, our convictions, and our sense of who we are. We must weave this new lesson into the very fabric of our character and self-expression.

This is what it means to apply the lessons of life.

The work of applying the lessons we learn can be condensed into a simple exercise. This exercise begins by reviewing a key character trait we have been striving to master—a trait such as patience, tolerance, cheerfulness, courage, self-discipline, or perseverance. Our goal is to examine how well we have learned and applied the lesson involved.

The first step is to determine the true message behind this lesson. If friends have betrayed us, the lesson to learn is not to distrust friends! The real message is to be faithful and true to our own ideals.

The second step is to determine what we intend to do about this problem—what changes in character and behavior will lead to an improvement.

The third step, then, is to define what the soul is striving to teach us, as opposed to what the personality wishes to learn. Our string of failed marriages is not designed to teach us to hate the opposite sex, after all, but rather to expose our own selfishness and deficiences. The lesson the soul is striving to teach us can usually be described in terms of a spiritual quality we lack, such as goodwill, patience, joy, or harmony.

Once we have defined the true lesson properly, then we must begin applying it. Once again three steps are involved:

1. How can we act with greater spiritual virtues in the struggles we are presently encountering?

2. How can we reenact episodes from the past in which we did not express as much spiritual strength as we should have? What negative emotional baggage—memories of shame, hurt, or anger—must we dissipate in order to restore health to our subconscious?

3. How can we integrate these new measures of spiritual strength into our values, our sense of identity, our creative skills, and our relationships with others? In the future, how will we cope with irritations, with setbacks, and even with failure? How will we deal with people who oppose us? How does this preview reset the compass of our priorities?

Consistent daily effort to apply the lessons we have learned throughout our life will steadily bring the personality more and more onto the wavelength of the soul. From that point on, we will view the learning process less as a burden and more as a daily communion with the very best within us.

14.

The Levels Of Learning

Many of the lessons we must learn in order to succeed in ordinary life are simple and easy to master. We do not have to understand the mechanics or design of an automobile in order to drive it; we simply must be able to learn the basic laws of the road and attain a practiced level of skill and confidence. Just so, lessons of politeness and etiquette can be learned by pure imitation—by mimicking our parents, for example. Even the ability to speak is a skill a child acquires by imitating adults.

The lessons involved in becoming a mature person—and then an agent of light—tend to be a bit more demanding. It is not possible to become a spiritual person just by imitating the outer appearance of a good example; if it were, then most agents of light by definition ought to ride donkeys and wear sandals and Middle Eastern garments.

The study of human psychology is, at the very least, rich and intricate. When seen as existing within a much larger context of light and spirit, then the process of learning expands into brave new dimensions we have not previously contemplated. The outer elements of life remain a significant part of our existence, of course, but their importance to us changes, as our focus and priorities in life shift more and more to the inner dimensions of consciousness.

For this reason, it is important to understand that the process of learning any lesson involves three distinct levels:

1. The initial stage of **imitation,** in which we mimic behavior we admire in others.

2. The second stage of **interaction,** in which we discover basic principles of living and then inaugurate improvements in our habits, priorities, and skills based on these discoveries.

3. The final stage of **integration,** in which we redefine our core values and the role we play as we implement this new ability or understanding through our behavior. It is at this level of learning that we tap the life and power of spirit for transformation. Indeed, until we reach this level, no permanent growth occurs. The two preliminary levels set the stage for the transformation in the third stage.

These three levels of learning are not always obvious at first, a factor that explains the discouragement often experienced by many would-be agents of light. These are good people who sincerely desire to grow, but have little inkling of the immense complexity of the lesson (or lessons) they have chosen to master. They work diligently on their problem of depression or their martyr complex for a few

174

months or years, making what seems to be substantial progress. At this point, they conclude erroneously that they have mastered the lesson at last, because they have learned to control their reactiveness, and the symptoms of depression or martyrdom have receded. But they have mastered only the first or second levels of learning. Eventually, new challenges storm into their life, bringing likewise a new wave of gloom or self-pity. In most cases, this new wave catches them so much by surprise that they may be overwhelmed by it. To them, it seems as if they have backslid and are worse off than ever. But this is just an illusion of the growth process; they are simply entering into the next phase of learning an important life lesson.

It is easiest to define these three levels of learning in terms of the comprehension of ideas. The act of becoming aware of an idea is not at all the same as understanding it. In fact, it often requires years (if not lifetimes) of exposure to important ideas before we begin to tap the full meaning and power behind them.

The three levels of learning about ideas can be described as follows:

1. We become aware of an idea and form a belief about its usefulness to us.

2. We begin to understand the function of the idea and how we can apply it.

3. We comprehend and embody the spiritual archetypal essence that is the power of this idea, in our character, our value system, and our self-expression.

A good example illustrating these levels of absorbing an

idea would be the concept of *freedom*. Freedom is one of the most commonly used and abused words in America. It is a word found in every political speech, even though it is most often invoked to deprive us of freedom rather than guarantee it.

When we first become aware of the concept of freedom, we tend to interpret it in highly personal terms. We view freedom as a natural right that protects us *from* certain evils—for example, too much governmental meddling in our affairs. But at this level, most people end up transmogrifying freedom into lots of things it is not—freedom from want, freedom from poverty, freedom from responsible behavior, freedom from punishment, and freedom from fault. Soon, they have blurred the word to the point where it has no real meaning at all. It has become a servant for propagandizing and brainwashing of others.

Of course, if we crave freedom from responsibility, we will gain it—so much of it, in fact, that we will soon tire of the limitations we have imposed on our life. Freedom from responsibility, after all, also creates a parallel condition of the absence of meaning, maturity, and accomplishment.

So our understanding of freedom begins to mature. Eventually, we will embark upon the second level of learning about freedom, in which we see it as the freedom *to do*—the freedom to be productive, to act wisely, to set and achieve goals, and to contribute to life. We begin to grasp that freedom without self-reliance, involvement, and responsibility is just a hollow deception.

Even this level of comprehension, however, imposes certain restrictions on us.   As we pursue various creative activities, we begin to find ourself trapped in conventions, traditions, and expectations.   We gradually recognize that there is still an element or dimension of freedom that we have not tapped. And so we strive to identify with freedom as the soul experiences it.   We examine the assumptions we—and society—have made about freedom, and then compare these ideas with the archetypal essence and design of freedom.   As we integrate these new insights into our awareness, we slowly revise our basic definition of freedom as well as the primary values and goals that have been shaped by our love for freedom.   We discover that the essence of freedom is actually the freedom *to be*—the full liberation of the light of the soul.

The same three levels of learning can be observed in our efforts to understand *love*.   At first, we personalize our use of love and think of this great energy as a feeling.   We feel the need for love, and establish this feeling as a high priority in our life.   We interpret love as a sense of fulfillment that nurtures and supports our well-being.   When this feeling is absent or withheld, we feel deprived emotionally, and so we crave the sensation of love even more.

Eventually, we come to realize that love is not as much a state of feeling as it is a verb—the capacity to nurture and give support to ourselves, others, and society.   Love nourishes the best within us and helps us bridge the gaps that appear in our journey of growth.   In this second phase of learning, we discover the love of the mature parent, who patiently cultivates the rich potential within his or her child, even when the child rebels.   We also discover that we can

177

love with the mind even more powerfully than with our feelings.

The third stage of learning about love takes us into the realm of spirit, where we discover that the true energy of love is an inclusive principle or force that connects us with the soul. The wavelength of love at this level of achievement is actually a super highway along which faith and commitment flow from the personality to the spirit, and healing, wisdom, and light flow from the soul into the personality.

The key to gaining mastery at this level of love is to practice and experience the inclusiveness and benevolence which are the keynotes of spiritual love, and to integrate them into our values, attitudes, and behavior.

The same three levels of learning apply to the acquisition of new or more refined skills in living. In this case, however, the description of the three levels is slightly different than with ideas:

1. The first level of imitation focuses on solving specific problems. It is often presented as a set of routines to be followed.

2. The second level of interaction teaches us to work with the basic principles that can solve entire classes of problems, not just individual cases.

3. The third level of integration leads to ability to create with these fundamental principles—the archetypes of spirit.

One of the skills of living that has been given a great deal of attention in modern times is the ability to communicate effectively with others. Unfortunately, the first lessons most people learn about communication are often counterproductive. We learn how to spread gossip and plant rumors. We learn how to express our hurt feelings, most notably our angry responses to insults. Even in listening to the news, we are drawn to sensationalism rather than substance.

The positive lessons we must learn at the first level, before we can move on, include knowing when to maintain silence instead of speaking, knowing how to speak *with* people instead of talking at them, and knowing how to listen effectively.

As these lessons are being learned, we enter into the second phase of mastering the art of communication. In this stage, we discover that issues and ideas are far more important than style and personality. A highly charismatic leader may fool most of the people for a long, long time, but eventually his or her lack of substance will be exposed. Just so, we need to make sure that the words we write or speak in communicating to others are clear expressions of substantive issues and insights. After all, an ability to communicate that is not linked to our values and principles creates the risk of misinforming or misleading.

As we link our ability to communicate with our basic values and principles, we are gradually drawn into the third stage of learning—the stage of learning to create with these principles and archetypal forces. At this level, of course, the skills of communication we must acquire tend to be nonverbal and abstract—the skills of spiritual telepathy. We must teach ourself how to identify with the love and wisdom of the soul and activate these forces in our own mind and heart, not just aspire to divine purity.

The same pattern can be discovered as we review the lessons involved in learning to pray effectively. To the average person, who has learned very little about the life of spirit except to fear it, prayer is an imitative art. The average person hears a priest or minister recite a prayer, and then copies what he or she hears verbatim, right down to the little throat-clearing noise between stanzas three and four! Little effort is made to understand the prayer or contact the forces it invokes, other than a general superstitious belief that this prayer will bring relief from some problem.

As our devotional life deepens, we learn that prayer is a great deal more profound. We begin to comprehend that the words themselves are not nearly as important as the attitude within our heart as we recite the prayer. And so, we learn to cultivate a state of deep devotion and genuine gratitude that serve to link us with spirit. We also begin to gain flashes of insight into the principles and dynamics of our prayers.

Yet it is only in the third phase of learning that the full power of prayer is discovered. In the second stage, we still preserve a sense of separation between us and spirit—between God "up there" and us "down here." As we interact with spirit through prayer and meditation, however, we gradually come to realize that there is no separation. When we pray, we seek to realize the presence of spirit within us and within all of life. Then we can pray for healing because our soul already is the essence of health. We can pray for relief from suffering—because our soul already exists within the grace of God.

As might be expected, the same three divisions in learning occur as we strive to refine our character and grow as a human being. In this regard, the three levels of learning can be listed as:

1. We strive to make changes in our character by restraining our outer behavior—through positive thinking, behavior modification, or imitation of a role model. Often, the effort to change becomes mostly a battle to *avoid* temptation or unpleasantness.

2. We inaugurate changes at our inner levels. Instead of just restraining our reactions, we set in motion new patterns, values, and priorities for acting, and strive to live up to them.

3. We draw upon the ideal patterns of the divine design for human living—the divine archetypes—and infuse these spiritual forces into every level of our character and self-expression. We express the saint within us.

An excellent example of the levels of learning in modifying our character would be the mastering of patience. At first, we tend to define patience simply as "waiting." In fact, we may even regard it as a character weakness—the inability to act decisively. Even if we try to become patient, we are apt to misinterpret it entirely and learn the wrong lesson, by turning off our feelings and becoming indifferent to the eventual outcome of some activity. We end up learning not to care, rather than acquiring genuine patience.

As we discover that we have misunderstood patience, we enter into the second stage of learning, where we practice intelligent self-discipline. We learn to wait until enough patterns and trends have unfolded in any given situation before we make a conclusive decision about action. Even more importantly, we train ourselves to see the larger issues that impetuous people overlook. Yet even this does not instill in us a perfect sense of patience. And so we move on to the third phase of learning, in which we learn to act with a sense of appropriateness—to act in accord with the patterns of the soul, regardless of time.

Another good example of these levels of learning as they relate to character growth would be the popular idea of the need for *assertiveness*. No one likes to be shoved around and manipulated by others. People who learn by imitation, however, are apt to try to correct this deficiency by copying the behaviors of those who control and dominate them. In other words, they become rude, pushy, and obnoxious in their attempt to balance out their innate passiveness, sweetness, and meekness. This does not make much sense. It merely trades in one set of flawed character qualities for an even more repulsive set.

The real problem of passiveness is not that other people abuse us, but that we never make the effort to express the best within us or dominate our environment. And so, we gradually begin to realize that assertiveness is actually the ability to be a positive influence on the life around us. We move on to the second level of learning, and strive to assert humanistic qualities, skills, and habits whenever possible. We discover that it is much more sensible to assert patience, kindness, and helpfulness than it is to assert pushiness, rudeness, or criticism.

The most subtle level of the process of becoming assertive, however, is the grand reversal of perspective and priority that leads us to being able to assert the soul in our everyday activities on earth. In order to learn this lesson, the personality must be able to heed the guidance and will of the soul while actively expressing wisdom, courage, and goodwill.

Once we understand that there are three distinct levels to any kind of learning, we can apply this knowledge to accelerate our own efforts to master any given lesson. By drawing on the archetypal patterns and principles of the life of spirit to guide us, we can shape our efforts to minimize the false starts that would hold us back in levels one and two.

In other words, if our goal is to become more patient, we can start our efforts by contemplating the divine design for patience—a subset of divine peace—instead of plunging into endless rounds of trial and error. We will still need to test what we learn, of course, but we can eliminate many of the problems that usually attend growth.

Indeed, this basic principle can become the foundation for another exercise. We begin by selecting an idea, skill, or quality of consciousness to perfect. The end result of phase three in the learning process will be the full embodiment of this idea, quality, or skill as a spiritual force. In this light, then, we should ask ourself:

"How well do I embody this idea, quality, or skill at

present? How will I know I am achieving growth? How must I proceed?"

In reviewing these questions, there are a number of key subordinate questions to ask and answer:

"How will this idea or principle influence my values and priorities?"

"How can I express this archetype in the way I interact with friends, colleagues, and loved ones?"

"How will it modify my sense of identity—of who I am?"

"How does embodying this force help me manage my daily problems and challenges?"

"How does learning this lesson enhance my relationship with God?"

ABOUT THE AUTHORS

In the late 1960's, Dr. Robert R. Leichtman's interest in intuition and spiritual growth caused him to close his medical practice and devote his energies to personal psychic work, lecturing, teaching, and writing. His pioneer work with psychiatrists, psychologists, and medical doctors has helped him become recognized as one of the best psychics in America today. Dr. Leichtman is also the developer of "Active Meditation," a comprehensive course in personal growth and meditative techniques. He is the author of the paperback series, *From Heaven to Earth*, published by Ariel Press, as well as *Fear No Evil* and *Recovering From Death*. Dr. Leichtman currently resides in Baltimore, where he continues the healing work of Olga Worrall at the New Life Clinic.

Carl Japikse grew up in Ohio. A graduate of Dartmouth College, he began his work career as a newspaper reporter with *The Wall Street Journal*. In the early 1970's, he left the field of journalism to teach personal and creative growth, lecture, and found Ariel Press. Mr. Japikse is the developer of "The Enlightened Management Seminar," "Write Light," and the "Enlightened Classroom," as well as various courses in spiritual growth, and the author of *The Light Within Us*, *Love Virtue*, *Exploring the Tarot*, *The Tarot Journal*, *The Hour Glass*, and *The Tao of Meow*.

Together, Dr. Leichtman and Mr. Japikse are the authors of *The Life of Spirit* and *The Art of Living* essay series, *Active Meditation*, *Forces of the Zodiac*, *Enlightenment*, and a four-book interpretation of the I Ching.

185

ENLIGHTENMENT

The Light of Learning is a compilation of 14 lessons on the process of learning from the *Enlightenment* series written by Robert R. Leichtman, M.D. and Carl Japikse and published by Ariel Press.

In addition to lessons on learning, the Enlightenment series deals with six other areas of enlightenment:

• *The Lights of Heaven*, an exploration of the archetypal forces of the mind of God.

• *The Revelation of Light*, which explores the nature of the psychic dimensions of life.

• *Embodying the Light*, a guide to enlightened self-expression and how it can enrich our lives.

• *Embracing the Light*, in which the process and techniques of spiritual integration are described.

• *The Light Which Penetrates*, an examination of the use of the mind to nourish itself on the wonderful advances of human civilization.

• *Our Companions in the Light* examines other forms of life on earth and how a reverence for the beauty and glory of all life enriches our own.

A new lesson is produced every two months and is sent to subscribers by first-class mail as they are ready. A subscription to one year (six) lessons is $18 postpaid.

Forty-two of the lessons have been written and distributed, as of the end of 1999. These 42—which include introductory lessons to each of the 7 themes of the series—can be purchased as a set for $90, postpaid.

Lessons 42 through 49 are being produced during 2000,

and sent to subscribers as they are ready.   The 6 lessons scheduled for 2000 are:

February—The Basis for Integration.

April—Tools of Integration.

June—Divine Archetypes in Music.

August—Archetypes in Divination.

October—Integrating Conduct with Intentions.

December—Integrating the Emotions with the Mind.

Lessons 49 to 54 will be produced during 2001.   They will examine:

February—Life as a Metaphor.

April—Archetypes in Science.

June—Archetypes in Government.

August—Archetypes in Education.

October—Archetypes in Art.

December—The Archetypes in Personal Growth.

The lessons are printed in a four-page, 8.5 by 11-inch format, pre-punched so that they can easily be collected in a three-ring binder.

To order the lessons already in print plus the 12 lessons being issued in 2000 and 2001, send a check or money order for $112 to Ariel Press at P.O. Box 297, Marble Hill, GA 30148. Or call toll free 1-800-336-7769 and charge the order to MasterCard, VISA, Discover, Diners, or American Express. Please call during our business hours, Tuesday through Thursday from 10 a.m. until 5 p.m. Eastern time. Or fax orders to 1 (706) 579-1865 anytime.

Additional copies of *The Light of Learning* are likewise available for $13.99 plus shipping ($4 for one book, $6 for two or more.)

OTHER BOOKS FROM ARIEL PRESS

BLACK LIGHT
A novel by Talbot Mundy, $10.95

THE ART OF LIVING
A five-volume set of essays
By Robert R. Leichtman, M.D. & Carl Japikse
$48

THE LIFE OF SPIRIT
A five-volume set of essays
By Robert R. Leichtman, M.D. & Carl Japikse
$50

FEAR NO EVIL
By Robert R. Leichtman, M.D., $9.95

LOVE VIRTUE
by Carl Japikse, $9.99

THE LIGHT WITHIN US
by Carl Japikse, $9.95

PRACTICAL MYSTICISM
by Evelyn Underhill, $9.95

THE GIFT OF HEALING
by Ambrose & Olga Worrall, $14.99